# A Prince Hall
# Masonic
# Quiz Book

# A Prince Hall Masonic Quiz Book

## by Joseph A. Walkes, Jr.

**REVISED AND ENLARGED EDITION**

*Originally published by the*
*Research Lodge No. 2 (White) of Ames, Iowa, 1983*

MACOY PUBLISHING & MASONIC SUPPLY CO., INC.
Richmond, Virginia

*Published by*
Macoy Publishing & Masonic Supply Co., Inc.
Richmond, Virginia


ISBN-0-88053-085-5

Printed in the United States of America

*This book is dedicated to*

KEITH ARRINGTON AND JERALD E. MARSENGILL
*of*
The Grand Lodge of Iowa, A.F. & A.M.

Two friends
And to
All Freemasons of Good Will

# Foreword to Second Edition

*"Other people see things and say why, but I dream of
things that never were, and I say, why not?"*

GEORGE BERNARD SHAW

In 1980 I was invited by Research Lodge No. 2 of Iowa, to
write this Quiz Book, as a means of bringing to their members an
educational look at Prince Hall Freemasonry. This was, as far as
I knew, the first time that a Prince Hall Freemason was to be
allowed to present his views in book form and have it published
by a "Caucasian" Masonic body. Macoy Publishing & Masonic
Supply Co., Inc. did publish *The Prince Hall Primer* by Harry A.
Williamson in 1949 and 1956 and my *Black Square and Com-
pass: 200 Years of Prince Hall Freemasonry* in 1981 as well as the
now discredited *Official History of Freemasonry among the Col-
ored People in North America* by William H. Grimshaw in 1903.
While on the other hand, the Most Worshipful Prince Hall
Grand Lodge of Massachusetts published in 1902, *Negro
Masonry being a Critical Examination of Objections to the
Legitimacy of the Masonry existing among the Negroes of
America* by William H. Upton of the Caucasian Grand Lodge of
Washington. However, this present Quiz Book was the first to be
published by a Research Lodge of mainstream Freemasonry.

This work, as well as others that I have penned, was an act of
love—love for the Royal Art. Often times my pen has caused me
to be misunderstood by those who I am sure carry the same love
of Freemasonry, but yet have not taken the time necessary to explore its varied subjects in greater detail.

Since I approach Freemasonry as a source of pleasure, I have
over two decades taken the time necessary to study in depth the
fascinating world of the Black Masonic Experience in America.

As in my other works, I have always tried to make it crystal
clear that I am not a spokesman for Prince Hall Freemasonry;

this is better left to the conservators of Ancient Craft Masonry—the Grand Masters. Sadly, I admit that in many instances, my works seem to be at odds with these leaders of the Craft—and often I can understand why they may take exceptions to some aspects of my writings. Often what I present is new and unheard of to them, while at the same time, it is well-known in Masonic research circles, outside of the Prince Hall fraternity.

Since the 1940's there have only been a few of us who have taken the time to attempt to fully explore this Masonic Power called Prince Hall Freemasonry and I must give my mentors credit, for they truly laid the ground work for my love of Masonic research. Harry A. Williamson, the "Grand Old Man of Prince Hall Freemasonry," who is quoted often in this work. Harry E. Davis of Ohio who was my first introduction to the history of our fraternity, and of course my dear friend, the link between the Black Renaissance period and Dr. W. E. B. DuBois and myself, the great historian, Dr. Charles H. Wesley. I have often said how tragic it has been that Caucasian Freemasonry for the most part has never been exposed to the great minds of Black Masonic America.

I want to express my appreciation to Macoy Publishing & Masonic Supply Co., Inc., and their willingness to republish this work as well as my *Black Square and Compass*, for they alone have made it possible for these works on Prince Hall Freemasonry to reach a countless number of Freemasons. In some cases they did not agree with some aspects of my writings, and for this I am sure they have received some criticism; but the fact remains that despite these negativies, they saw a need and stepped in and published my works anyway. I will always be grateful to them and their President H. Paul Scholte.

A special "thank you" to Jerry Marsengil, of Research Lodge No. 2, and the Editor of *The Philalethes Magazine* and the *Royal Arch Mason Magazine*. Jerry and I seldom agree, but we have been friends for over a decade. His interest in Prince Hall Freemasonry has, to me, always been genuine and sincere and his book *Negro Masonry in Iowa* stands as a beacon to that interest. Thanks also to Research Lodge for having the fortitude to first publish this Quiz Book even though some of their members were against it.

Finally, my appreciation for my beloved Prince Hall Freemasonry, which for more than 200 years has been ridiculed and abused, called irregular and clandestine, often by men not fit to call themselves Freemasons; yet, Prince Hall Freemasonry has stood fast and firm, holding its head high, and continuing to practice the Royal Art surpasing even the greatness of the Mother Grand Lodge which gave it birth and then turned its back and pretended that It was not one of its daughters.

Through it all, the true hero, has been Prince Hall and the Craftsmen of African Lodge No. 459 who have passed on Freemasonry and made it a part of the Black Experience in America. The heritage continues, and I am proud to be a part of it.

JOSEPH A. WALKES, JR.

Leavenworth, Kansas
January, 1989

# The Reason for this Book

Truthfully, it can certainly be said that I am not an "official" spokesman for Prince Hall Freemasonry, and I would be the first to agree. The Prince Hall fraternity, without a doubt, has able and capable prolocutors, who can make the official stance of the Prince Hall family known, such as the Conference of Prince Hall Grand Masters.

Nevertheless, as an individual that has a true love of Freemasonry on the one hand, and as a concerned American citizen on the other, I would like to see in my life time a solution to American Freemasonry's most vexing and disturbing problem—what to do about the Black American and his Masonry. Therefore, in this area of great concern, I would like to add my voice and my views.

For two hundred years, American Freemasonry has been plaqued by this division of its Craft. "What is still more remarkable," wrote Rev. John Eliot back in 1795, "white and black masons do not sit together in their lodges." Today in 1983, as we witness a decline in Freemasonry and its influence, the *status quo* remains and the division along racial lines continues. Indeed, it is shocking to learn that Freemasonry is the most segregated institution in America. And for two hundred years, the pros and cons have been debated by numerous personalities in support of and against this festering problem, that, like a cancer, continues eating away at the body of Freemasonry.

When American Freemasonry can be compared by the non-Masonic public as comparable to the Ku Klux Klan and other tragic groups of hate, surely we have a problem. It is an American problem, that can only be solved by Americans who are willing and have the best interest of American Freemasonry in their hearts.

I, therefore, recommend that the following be considered. For the lack of a better name, I call it the Walkes Blue-print!

1. There must be an immediate ceasation of hostile articles, papers and books that are considered abusive to either fraternity; for its continuation breeds nothing but pure racial hatred! While it is understood that there will be individuals who will intensify their efforts to hinder any accord, they must not be given any offical sanction from the leadership of either body.

2. That the individual Caucasian State Grand Lodges with the *concurrence* of its State Prince Hall Grand Lodges, accept quietly and without fan-fare "as is," as Provincial Grand Lodges, the State Prince Hall Grand Lodges, thereby allowing the Prince Hall brethren to maintain their separate identity and continue with the blessing and respect of their Caucasian counterparts, who may feel a need to maintain the purely American Doctrine of Territorial Jurisdiction. The Prince Hall Craft to continue along its individual path, as a member of the Universal Masonic family, and time will eventually heal the breach more fully, and the family will one day become one, thus ending the long night of Masonic nightmare.

3. Appoint Grand Lodge Representatives to the Provincial Grand Lodges and accept representatives from the Prince Hall Craft, thus establishing the means to have permanent dialogue and to solve problems as they arise.

4. Open up and combine Masonic homes, hospitals, libraries to all Freemasons of the Grand and Provincial Grand Lodges, the cost to be shared upon the total membership of each.

5. The conference of Grand Masters of both fraternities to meet jointly annually to establish working committees whereby joint areas of interest can be addressed for the good of the entire community and the fraternity.

6. On the state level, establish joint educational seminars together, and join together in common tables whenever possible.

7. No interference from other houses of Freemasonry or other Masonic jurisdictions should be permitted.

We can continue divided and wither away and die in our shame, or come together as American citizens and solve our problems once and for all, with mutual respect for each other, and continue our progress as ono family, united, under the banner of Universal Freemasonry.

# Table of Contents

PART                                                                      PAGE

*Foreword* . . . . . . . . . . . . . . . . . . . . . . . . . . . . . . . . . . . . .     *vii*

*The Reason for this Book* . . . . . . . . . . . . . . . . . . . . . .     *xi*

*Introduction* . . . . . . . . . . . . . . . . . . . . . . . . . . . . . . . . .     *xvii*

PART ONE—
Prince Hall and African Lodge . . . . . . . . . . . . . . . . .     1

PART TWO—
The Formation of the Prince Hall
    Grand Lodges . . . . . . . . . . . . . . . . . . . . . . . . . . . . . .     33

PART THREE—
The "National Grand Lodge" . . . . . . . . . . . . . . . . . . .     56

PART FOUR—
The Damning of Saint Orgne . . . . . . . . . . . . . . . . . . .     78

PART FIVE—
Of The Craft and Things . . . . . . . . . . . . . . . . . . . . . .     95

Addendum—
The Phylaxis Society . . . . . . . . . . . . . . . . . . . . . . . . . .     147

# Introduction
## by Jerry Marsengill

When I began my book on *Negro Masonry in Iowa*, I made the statement that no class of people was more ignorant about Prince Hall Masonry than the average white Freemason. I also stated that, if there were others more ignorant about the subject, these others were Prince Hall Freemasons.

In seventeen years I have found little reason to change my opinions. The only difference is that now, far too many of these are finding it necessary to display their ignorance in print.

The subject of Prince Hall Freemasonry is a thorny one. One cannot find much hard evidence to prove any particular contention. The few records which exist cannot be depended on. One such record is the minute book of African Lodge. Recently a spate of books has been issued, many of which depend on these minutes to make some particular point. Since the minutes were rewritten (and most probaby altered) by John Hilton, it is difficult to use them as a source of good evidence.

Another case concerns the manumission certificate which appeared originally in the *Philalethes Magazine*. It is a copy of the original which was made by Ezekiel Price for his records. As far as I personally know, no one has seen the original. Regardless of this, if the certificate is a true and exact copy, it does not prove that the certificate was issued to the "Masonic" Prince Hall. More than one man named Prince Hall resided in and around Boston at that time.

Contrary to the opinion expressed in this book, I believe that Prince Hall was most probably a slave. My main reason for so thinking is the name. Prince was not a name given by Africans. It was a favorite name with white slaveowners, many of whom named their favorite slaves Prince, King, Rex, Pompey, Caesar or some other high sounding royal appelation. This was done in the same manner that a horse or a dog would be given some distinctive kennel name.

This is a book which is intended to give white Masons some insight into the way typical black Freemasons view the fraternity. It should also be educational to the members of the Prince Hall Affiliation. Some of the author's conclusions will be offensive to both blacks and whites. Most of the facts will surprise many people.

While editing the book, I found myself offended at some of the statements and some of the quotations. I was especially disturbed when Louis Block, one of my Masonic heroes, was quoted as saying, in effect, that Negroes were not mentally or morally qualified to be Freemasons. When I looked up the reference I was even more disturbed at Block, not at Bro. Walkes. He said it.

I also disagree with Bro. Walkes on some of his quotations from the Proceedings of various Grand Lodges. I do believe that the people who wrote these were creatures of their times and that they expressed the prevailing sentiment of their times. I further believe that more men of good will exist on either side of the color line than Walkes admits. We have white bigots. I readily admit that. I also have met a number of black bigots. But, among Masons, I have met more men of good will, both black and white, than I have ever met racists.

When Keith Arrington, William Durow and I attended the tenth anniversary of the Phylaxis Society in Minneapolis, they made a strong case for recognition. I am convinced that they have many of the genuine secrets of Freemasonry. Their banquet served the same roast beef, potatoes and green beans for which our white banquets are noted. Their introductions were just as lengthy, their titles, both Past and Present, as ostentatious and their speeches as tedious as any of ours. If they do not know all about Masonry, they certainly know a great deal. When a banquet can begin at 6:30 PM and end at 10:15 PM, you know you are among Masons.

The publication of this book was not my suggestion. I am careful never to involve Research Lodge No. 2 or the Grand Lodge of Iowa in any crusade which I may have at any particular time. This book was suggested at one of our regular meetings and it was the concensus of opinion of the officers and members present that our membership should know more about Prince Hall Freemasonry. Bro. Walkes was suggested as the author and the book has grown since that time.

Walkes has done a magnificent job. The book is abrasive. In many respects it is controversial. To those of closed minds it will be offensive. But, to thinking men, both black and white, it will be a revelation. Walkes does not pull any punches. He criticizes the Prince Hall fraternity as readily as he does the white fraternity. If you read it with an open mind, you will learn a great deal not only about black Masonry but about the way a black man thinks of Masonry. In the words of William H. Upton, P.G.M. of Washington, it will cast some "light on a dark subject."

# PART ONE

# Prince Hall and African Lodge

1. **Prince Hall Freemasonry is named after Prince Hall. Who was Prince Hall?**

   There continues to be a lack of information concerning the life of Prince Hall. This is a subject of much speculation within Masonic circles. Many questions remain unanswered. It is estimated from newspaper accounts of his death that he was born about 1735. The place of his birth is unknown. Some have speculated that he was born in Barbados, West Indies. There is no evidence to support this.[1] Others have claimed Africa as his place of birth,[2] while still others say he was born in the United States.[3]

   Documents that have survived show him to be a laborer,[4] a leather dresser[5] and a caterer[6]. Other documentation shows him to be a voter who was without a doubt a leader within the small Black community in Boston, Massachusetts.

2. **What is the traditional version of the life of Prince Hall and where did it come from?**

   The traditional version unfortunately is widely accepted but it does not hold up to research. It was first penned by Past Grand Master William H. Grimshaw of Washington, D.C.. He allowed his imagination to have free rein. He wrote that Prince Hall was born in Bridgetown, Barbados, West Indies in 1748, a son of Thomas Hall, an Englishman, a leather merchant, whose wife was a free Negro woman of French descent. He came to New England during the middle of the eighteenth century, settling in the City of Boston, in the Massachusetts colony where he became a minister of the

1

gospel, with the Methodist Church. However, none of this has withstood proper investigation.[7]

### 3. On what did Grimshaw base his facts?

He claimed that he took the information off of a headstone in Barbados,[8] but in reality he took the information for the year of birth from the *Massachusetts Soldiers and Sailors in the Revolution,* using the name of the Prince Hall from Medford, subtracting the age listed from the date of enlistment, as well as the height which is listed at 5 feet 3 inches. The remainder he concocted.

### 4. Did Prince Hall serve in the Revolutionary Army?

It must be understood that there were a number of Blacks by the name of Prince Hall residing in and around Boston and a number of them are listed on the rolls as having served in the Revolutionary Army. It is this writer's contention that the evidence does not support the claim that the Masonic Prince Hall served in the Revolutionary Army.[9]

### 5. There is some question of Prince Hall being a slave.

In 1963, John Sherman of Massachusetts, writing in *The Philalethes* recorded the following document:

> This may certify it may concern that Prince Hall has lived with us 21 (date unclear may be 25) years and served us well upon all occasions for which reasons we maturely give him his freedom and that he is no longer to be Rechoned a slave but has been always accounted as a freeman by us as he has served us faithfully upon that account we have given him his freedom as Witness our hands this ninth day of April 1770.
>
> Witnesses                                       William Hall
> Susannah Hall                                   Margarett Hall
> X Elizabeth Hall's mark
>      Boston 12 April 1770. Recorded[10]

There are, however, a number of problems with this document. First, it is not a "true copy" but rather a copy or transcript for the diary purpose of Ezekiel Price for his own non-official personal records. The term "maturely" would, to this writer, mean at age 21, which would make his date of birth 1749. If 25, the date of birth would be 1745, neither squaring with the newspaper accounts of his death. In the words of Harold A. Wilson, Grand Historian of the Prince Hall Grand Lodge of New York, "it is all incredible, absurd and ridiculous." It is this writer's contention that slavery was a part of the life and times of Black America and as Mahatma Gandhi wrote in a letter to Bro. W.E.B. DuBois in 1929 "Let not the 12 million Negroes be ashamed of the fact that they are the grand-children of the slaves. There is no dishonour in being slaves. There is dishonor in being slave-owners."[11]

Slavery is the illegal kidnapping of human beings, and the illegal holding into bondage of same. Prince Hall Freemasonry has never accepted this, and has never denied into membership ex-slaves. The Grand Lodge of England, after the abolition of slavery in the West Indies by the British Parliament on September 1, 1847, changed the word *free-born* to *free man* for entry into its lodges.[12]

6. **In the answer to question No. 1 it is mentioned that Prince Hall was a leader. What were some of his activities?**

He, together with several others, addressed a petition protesting against the existence of slavery in the Colony to the Massachusetts legislature. This document was dated January 13, 1777. He, with others, also forwarded a petition to the legislature protesting against the kidnapping and subsequent sale into slavery of a number of Blacks who had been kidnapped and taken from Boston on a ship to the West Indies. The petition was dated February 27, 1788. The men were returned to Boston after being detained by the Governor of Maine who complied with the request of the Governor of Massachusetts.[13]

7. **When and how did Prince Hall become a Mason?**

This is not definitely known as documentation showing dates have not been found. Tradition has it that he was initiated March 6, 1775. The famed historian, Dr. Jeremy Belknap, wrote "Having once and again mentioned this person (Prince Hall), I must inform you that he is grand master of a Lodge of free masons, composed wholly of blacks, and distinguished by the name of the 'African Lodge'. It was begun in 1775, while this town was garrisoned by British troops; some of whom held a lodge, and initiated a number of negroes. After the peace, they sent to England, and procured a charter under the authority of the Duke of Cumberland, and signed by the late Earl of Effingham."[14] Harry E. Davis, in his history of Prince Hall Freemasonry, wrote that Hall had been initiated in Lodge No. 441 which was a military lodge working under the Grand Lodge of Ireland and attached to one of the regiments in the Army of General Gage, and that the Master was a "Brother J. B. Batt."[15]

It is difficult to ascertain the validity of this. The minutes of African Lodge which have survived raise as many questions as they answer. Prince Hall Freemasonry accepts that date and counts its beginning from that time. Much confusion exists concerning that period. Blacks were formerly uneducated, being restricted by law from acquiring an education, with "Black codes" legally restricting more than two or three Blacks from assembling or holding meetings. To put the entire period in proper perspective one would need to understand the racial conditions of the time."[16] One can not judge the events of the period in the same context as one judges the early beginning of the Caucasian Colonist. While present, Blacks lived in a different "time frame" in Colonial America than their Caucasian counterparts. This concept requires a rethinking for all those who would judge Prince Hall Freemasonry.[17]

8.    **What became of Lodge 441?**

In due course it moved from the vicinity of Boston to New York State[17] and became one of the Lodges which participated in the formation of the First Caucasian Grand Lodge.

9. **With the removal of the Lodge, did Prince Hall and his Brethren have Masonic covering?**

In this, we have the words of Prince Hall, that Brother J. B. Batt had left them with what was known at the time as a "permit." Today we use the term "dispensation" in the United States, though England does not use this usage or terminology. There is much controversy surrounding this entire period, there has yet to be found documentation to support or to discredit the statement of Prince Hall. However, all of this is moot, as the actions of the Grand Lodge of England gave its "blessings" to the entire proceedings.

10. **What did the "permit" authorize Prince Hall and his Brethren to do?**

All that is known from Prince Hall's statement was that they were given the right to assemble and to bury their dead. The document, if actually given, has not survived, and one can not be sure that it did not grant the Blacks the full privilege of Masonry. The permit may have been verbal. Who is to say?

11. **Was Prince Hall initiating members?**

It is a possibility. It must be stressed that the minutes of the Lodge that have survived leave much to be desired. One must consider the times, and the Black/White condition of the period, wherein we are dealing with two distinctly different Americas. It is this writer's contention that whatever Prince Hall and the early members of the African Lodge did to survive, while not fully in accord with the strict confines of Masonic jurisprudence, was justified. Their actions were no better nor no worse than those of their Caucasian counterparts, who, more times than not, developed their organizations adopting innovations as it pleased them. Is it fair to judge Prince Hall and his Brethren by a standard of regularity to which none of the "mainstream" Grand Lodges in the United States could conform and which would render all Freemasonry irregular outside of the Mother Grand Lodge of England?

12. **Did Prince Hall or any of the members of African Lodge petition for recognition to the Caucasian Jurisdiction of Massachusetts?**

Yes, according to Prince Hall, a petition was sent to Provincial Grand Master Joseph Warren for Masonic recognition. It was received. However, Joseph Warren was killed at the Battle of Bunker Hill before it could be acted upon. It is interesting to note that with the death of Warren, the Caucasian Jurisdiction of Massachusetts ended, and there was no legal Masonic authority.[18]

13. **What other documents from the hands of Prince Hall survived?**

There are a number. The two charges to African Lodge are included (1792 and 1797). One is considered the first published address by a Black American, though another member of African Lodge may hold this honor.[19] Prince Hall's letter book has also survived, and is one of the most prized documents within Prince Hall Freemasonry.[20]

14. **Prince Hall petitioned the Grand Lodge of England for a warrent. When was this?**

It seems that Prince Hall was encouraged to apply to the Grand Orient of France for recognition.[21] He ignored this advice and applied to the fountain of Freemasonry, the Grand Lodge of England through Brother William M. Moody of Lodge of Brotherly Love No. 55, later Master of Perseverance Lodge No. 298, in two letters. The first was dated March 2, 1784 and the second June 30, 1784. The petition was successful and the Grand Lodge of England (Moderns) issued a warrant to African Lodge No. 459 on September 20, 1784.[22] With this authorization, any irregularity of the Blacks ceased. While a number of Masonic writers have questioned the granting of the warrant, it must be recognized that the Mother Grand Lodge of Freemasonry was not about to grant warrants to just anyone. It must have been assured that Prince Hall and his Brethren were authorized to receive the warrants. The charter reached Prince Hall April 29, 1787 and was recorded in the local newspapers.[23]

The charter remains in the hands of the Prince Hall Grand Lodge of Massachusetts. In 1869, it was singed in a fire, but was saved by the action of P.G.M. Kendall who retrieved the document.[24] There are a number of Prince Hall Freemasons who believe that the fire was an attempt by Caucasian Freemasonry to destroy this most prized of all documents of Prince Hall Freemasonry.[25] While this belief cannot be proved, the fact that it is held shows the often strained relationship between the Prince Hall fraternity and its Caucasian counterpart. It also shows the emotional connection of Black and White America.

15. **What was the relationship between African Lodge and the Grand Lodge of England?**

It seems to be extraordinarily good as Prince Hall did remain in contact with the Grand Lodge, giving reports on a number of Lodges in the area. All of which raised a number of questions, none of which has ever been fully explained. How was Prince Hall, an uneducated Black Man living in difficult times in Colonial America, able to establish the Masonic contacts that he did? Surely there is more to this than meets the eye.[26]

African Lodge made a number of contributions to the English Grand Charity Fund. They were:

| | |
|---|---|
| November 24, 1787 | $10.00 |
| November 25, 1789 | 2/2/11 |
| April 18, 1792 | 1/1/10 |
| November 27, 1793 | 1/5/6 |
| November 22, 1797 | 1/5/0 |

16. **What can be said of the minutes of African Lodge?**

A considerable amount of misunderstanding exists concerning the surviving records of African Lodge. Many of the early records of the Lodge were reported by the Caucasian

Grand Lodge of Massachusetts as having been destroyed by fire.[28]

What follows is recorded in the surviving minutes and has created quite a stir within Masonic research circles:

Prince Hall—Grand Marster 1778
Thomas Saunderson, Secretary—Maid Master 1778
Prince Taylor—Maid Marster May 30th 1778
Bristall Slinser—Maid Marster May 30th 1778
Cyris Forbs—Maid Marster June 2th 1778
Petter Betts—Made Marster June 20th 1778
    Decest 1778
Forton Howard—Maid marster May 14th 1779
Luke Belchard—maid marster May 28 1779
Lanchester Hill—maid marster June 23, 1779
    Treasurer
Prince Reed—maid marster June 23, 1779
Jube Hill—maid marster January 26, 1781
May 2 (1781) Boston Smith, Witt Grigery,
    Quentes Gill, Ceser Spear.[29]

More than ample evidence exists that the minutes of African Lodge were poorly written by John T. Hilton. This was recorded by Brother Jacob Norton in a letter to Brother John D. Caldwell which most critics of Prince Hall Freemasonry have ignored.[30]

To further illustrate how unreliable the rewritten minutes of African Lodge are, they record the date of death for Prince Hall incorrectly and use such terms as "being raised to the Sublime Degree of Master Mason" when that term was not used until 1817.[31] It is clear that the rewritten minutes of African Lodge cannot be used as basis for Masonic research. They have been proved to be completely unreliable.

17. **It is alleged that African Lodge was dormant for a length of time.**

Evidence to the contrary exists.[32]

18. **Did African Lodge of Boston possess the right and power to form itself into a Grand or Mother Lodge?**

By today's standards, *no.* Here again it must be understood, that we are dealing with a "nation within a nation" in the midst of a hostile mainstream which by its very laws was attempting to keep the Black inferior, uneducated and subservient. There were a number of other Masonic bodies who used similar procedures as African Lodge.[33]

### 19. Prince Hall died in 1807, give some information.

Most Worshipful Brother Prince Hall, the first Black man known to have received the degrees of Freemasonry in America, passed away December 4, 1807. His death was recorded in a number of newspapers in Boston. The newspapers were dated December 7th, and hence it has been erroneously recorded that his death was on this date.[34]

Tradition has it that Hall was buried in Copps Hill Burial ground. A few note that there is no record of internment.[35] Copps Hill was the property of a Black by the name of William Copp.[36] Sarah Ritchey, one of the wives of Prince Hall, was buried in Copps Hill, and carved behind her tombstone reads:

> "Here lies ye body of
> Prince Hall
> First Grand Master of the
> Colored Grand Lodge of
> Masons in Mass.
> Died Dec. 7, 1807"

### 20. How does Prince Hall Freemasonry honor the memory of its founder?

Each year in September, Prince Hall Freemasonry holds a public ceremony, usually in a church, known as "Prince Hall Americanism Day." Like the Saints John, Prince Hall is considered the "Patron Saint" of the fraternity named after him. Most Lodges carry a "likeness" of Prince Hall, and every ten years, the Conference of Prince Hall Grand Masters holds a pilgrimage to Boston at the memorial shaft in his honor at Copps Hill.

In Philadelphia a Prince Hall Elementary School is named in honor of the first Black Freemason, and across America, there are a number of housing projects built with the help of the U.S. Government, and sponsored by the individual Grand Lodges, named after Prince Hall.

Many of the Prince Hall Grand Lodges feature a facsimile of the warrant of African Lodge No. 459 and a "likeness" of Prince Hall in the front of their proceedings.

In commemoration of the 200th Anniversary of Prince Hall Freemasonry, a number of the Grand Lodges minted special medallions as well as postage seals with a "likeness" of Prince Hall. The Phylaxis Society, an international research society of Prince Hall Freemasons holds its annual meetings close to March 6th, and publishes a special edition of its *Phylaxis* magazine in March, both in honor of Prince Hall.

Prince Hall will always be revered by the fraternity named after him.

## Notes for Part One

1. William H. Grimshaw, *Official History of Freemasonry Among the Colored People in North America* (New York, Books for Libraries Press, 1971) p. 69.

2. Alphonse Cerza, *The Prince Hall Organization* (June 9, 1980, presented before the South Dakota Lodge of Research) In an article by Harold V. B. Voorhis (1969) *Freemasonry Among Colored Men in America—Thumb-nail Sketch of the Advent—1775 Plus* (authors collection) "As we don't know when or where he was born, it is silly to speculate on his parents being one white and the other black. Grimshaw was a bastard himself, part black and part white, too, so he probably decided that Prince Hall should be too." Both of these men, by the very nature of the insensitivity of their writings towards Blacks, have created bitter feelings towards (regular) Freemasonry among Prince Hall Freemasons, and their works have been dismissed as biased. Using the January 14, 1787, Petition of African Blacks to General Court for aid in establishing an African colony (Mass. State Archives—African Petition 2358. H. of R. Journals VII, 381) (Prince Hall signed the document) as their basis, there are those who believe that Hall's place of birth was Africa. This is due to the lack of knowledge of the Black man. It must be remembered that during the period in question the term "Negro" was seldom used by Blacks or anyone else; and so such terms as "The African Church," "The African School," or "The African Lodge" were more in keeping with what Blacks considered themselves, however, the term "African" was never meant to imply that any were in fact born in Africa. Today many Blacks call themselves "Afro-American."

3. William H. Upton, *Prince Hall's Letter Book* (Transactions of the Quatuor Coronati Lodge, 1900, A.Q.C., 13, London) "Negro Masons in Maryland have claimed him—on what authority, if any, I know not—as a son of that colony; and a single word in one of his own letters

might lead some to look to England for his nativity." The letter mentioned by Upton reads: "Reports received into the Lodge since August two members, namely John Bean and John Marrant, a black minister from *Home...*" (see item 21, Upton above). This writer agrees with Upton, that there is a very good chance that Prince Hall was from England for it seems strange that an uneducated Black man living in Boston during that time could have had the contacts in England that Prince Hall obviously had.

4. Suffolk County Registry of Deeds—1807, August 31, Prince Hall Grantor—Deposition of Prince Hall concerning John Vinall, member of Church of the Rev. Andrews Croswell on School Street, Vol. 221, p.10.

5. On August 31, 1807, four months before he died, Prince Hall made a sworn deposition for John Vinal, a member of the Church of the Rev. Andrew Crosell, "I, Prince Hall of Boston in the County of Suffolk, Leather Dresser..." see Joseph A. Walkes, Jr., *"Black Square & Compass: 200 Years of Prince Hall Freemasonry"* (Virginia, Macoy Publishing Co., 1981) p. 7

6. In the Diary of William Bentley, D.D., Pastor of the East Church in Salem, a Freemason, see Charles H. Wesley, *Prince Hall: Life and Legacy* (Washington, United Supreme Council, A.A.S.R., S.J., P.H.A. & The Afro-American Historical & Cultural Museum) p. 89

7. Walkes, *op cit*, p. 8

8. Harry E. Davis, *A History of Freemasonry Among Negroes in America,* (United Supreme Council, AASR, NJ, PHA, 1946) p. 226

9. Walkes, *op cit.,* 9-10. An interesting paper on the subject in the writer's collection is by John M. Sherman, the Grand Historian of the Grand Lodge of Massachusetts, *"Prince Hall of Boston, the Freemason, was not a Revolutionary War Soldier—Records show two other Negroes from Medford, Mass., were the Veterans."* Masonically, it is immaterial whether or not Prince Hall served in the Revolutionary War, it has no bearing whatever on his Lodge or Prince Hall Freemasonry.

10. A letter from Harold A. Wilson, the Grand Historian of the Prince Hall Grand Lodge of New York, dated March 1, 1965 in this writer's collection may be of some interest:

> Author Sherman makes much over a document which he procured from the Boston Athenaeum and as contained with the Price Notarial Records, and which he alleges is the

Author Sherman makes much over a document which he procured from the Boston Athenaeum and as contained with the Price Notarial Records, and which he alleges is the manumission certificate of *Prince Hall, the Founder of Negro Freemasonry in America.* Now I do not doubt or have argument with the authenticity or credibility of the original document *per se,* conceded; but the conclusions deduced or drawn from the memorial by Sherman, in stark and chilling contrast of truth, I do. It would just seem that the whole of the Sherman thinking proceeds and motivates from the premise that the Hall indicated in the manumission certificate was the only Prince Hall to reside in Boston contemporary to the general period in question, and accordingly, was/is the one commonly known and referred to as the Founder of Negro Freemasonry in America. I take exception!

I note that the recorded date of the represented manumission should have been "1770" and not "1779". The line which reads "At the Boston Athenium" is not a part of the document and should read "Athenaeum." The Anthenaeum, 10½ Beacon Street, Boston, is one of the oldest existing proprietary libraries in the United States. Inaccuracies noted above reflect the sloppy and careless type work of the author and a certain lack of attention to detail.

*Writer's Note:* The notary Ezekiel Price (c. 1728-1802) was a native of Boston. He was the secretary for three Colonial governors of Massachusetts, viz: William Shirley, Thomas Pownall, and Sir Francis Bernard. In addition to being a Notary Public, Price was Clerk of the Courts of Common Pleas and Sessions, both before and after the Revolutionary War, Registrar of Deeds of Suffolk County, an insurance broker, and a Selectman of Boston for over thirty years (The New England Historical and Genealogical Register, Boston, 1865, 19:329-331).

*Writer's Note:* It has been my thinking for some several years if we could locate a listing of proprietary libraries or in some manner be able to identify them, research into the personality of Prince Hall and Negro Freemasonry would receive a jumbo shot in the arm.

Under the date of 5 December 1963 the Boston Public Library informed:

"There does not seem to be a list of proprietary Libraries either in the Commonwealth of Massachusetts or in the

United States in the directories owned by this Library. The American Library Directory lists libraries by State and City, alphabetically, without regard to the public or private nature of the institution."

I have additional correspondence on this matter which is not readily at hand.

In the *Philalethes Magazine,* issue of April 1963, Sherman asserts (I presume in new evidence):

> In the official "History of Freemasonry Among the Colored People in North America" by William H. Grimshaw, which for many years was accepted as fact, on page 69, it is stated that Prince Hall was born in Barbados and at the age of seventeen came to Boston in 1765. It is obvious, from the above document (re manumission certificate), that Prince Hall was in Boston as early as 1749.

That the Founder of Negro Freemasonry was in Boston in 1749 is an incredible, absurd and ridiculous fabrication and allegation by Sherman. His sense, and what there is of it, is deduced from a single piece of flimsy evidence as represented in a record of a record of a manumission certificate, by which *one, if he chooses,* may presume (a presumption is only a presumption) through deduction that a "Prince Hall" probably was in Boston in 1749. Let's keep in mind that date is not historical fact. Now it would only seem to appear that a "Prince Hall" was in Boston in 1749—the "Prince Hall," *no!* Can Sherman support with *proof-fact* that the William Hall family and slave Prince resided and did live in fact in Boston in 1749 as he asserts in his *premise?* Can he produce documents or papers supporting acquisition of slave Prince by William Hall family in 1749? Can he? If he, Sherman, can't produce any of the said documents and proof, he ought to go tell his thinking on a mountain, somewhere, where only he can hear it! Sherman fails to note in his article that there were several contemporary "Prince Halls" residing in or around Boston, a fact which he very well knows. Considerable cumulative evidence (public record) available to the personalities of the several "Prince Halls," I should think, can well serve to refute and destroy Sherman's allegation. I am torn in intellectual disbelief when I realize that he has most outrageously disregarded the several "Prince Hall" personalities. Almost it appears, that Sherman reached into a "hat," selected the personality suitable to his somewhat twisted ends, and proceeded "hell-bent" in purpose. It is quite obvious, too, that coupled with his effort to promiscuously assign a date to the appearance of Hall in Boston, Sherman is determined to allege that the

Founder of Negro Freemasonry was a slave which automatically raises the "free-born" question. As I reject his allegations that Hall was a slave, it is unnecessary for me to treat the theory.

Upon receipt of certain excerpts, I wrote to a close friend and colleague, D. O. Braithwaite, under date of 5 September 1960:

> "Herein enclosed are photostatic copies of the Revolutionary War service of *soldiers* named *Prince Hall*. They are excerpts from the *Massachusetts Soldiers and Sailors of the Revolutionary War*, an official publication by the Office of the Secretary of the Commonwealth.
>
> In order to be intellectually honest, it should be established as a fact, whether one, two, or all of the service records here submitted or to be submitted belongs to our "hero." You and I both know that there were more than one Prince Hall all who resided in Boston (the directories reveal this).

Dan replied 10 Sept. 1960, in part:

> Little did we know that our "hero" Prince Hall could have been an illusive or double character until recently, and it is fortunate for us at this time to know the facts—if any in our day.

From the above one can deduce that we were some time ago aware that there were several "Prince Halls" contemporary to our "hero." Such knowledge caused no great stir or sense of intellectual crisis. Our only purpose then and now was/is to be intellectually honest. The same cannot be said of Sherman.

On July 30, 1963, I communicated with the Massachusetts Historical Society, requesting certain information pertaining to the manumission of slaves. Under date of August 2 (note the time gap), John D. Cushing, an Assistant Librarian replied, in part, to wit:

> There is no agency of the Commonwealth that can furnish you with the information you seek. The difficulty, primarily, is that there were never any formal manumission proceedings by any agency of government.
>
> The subject came before the General Court on serveral occasions, but the difficulty standing in the way of formal emancipations seems to have been the status of old slaves who were no longer able to work. To have relieved their masters of obligations to support them would have meant a new class of town wards would appear, and citizens of the Commonwealth were most assiduous in keeping the class to a minimum.
>
> If any single agency may be credited with emancipation, it is the Massachusetts Supreme Judicial Court, in the actions of

Caldwell vs. Jennison, Worcester Session, April Term, 1783. Neither of these cases has been reported and the manuscript record is incomplete.

I am enclosing an article of mine that embodies the essentials of several years research and which, I understand and believe, is the most definitive study yet done. I have made every attempt to make it so. Meanwhile, research on this and allied subjects continues. I have amassed a considerable bulk of additional data, none of which changes the basic conclusions as stated in this article. If I uncover anything that might seriously modify the matter I will, if you wish, send along to you.

I acknowledged Cushing's letter, at the same time, requesting information as to the manumission of a "Prince Hall" in 1770. Now the gentleman's letter to me covered two pages and his article was 27 pages in length. As he went to the extent of furnishing me his article, indicated he would furnish additional material, and freely expressed the opinion that his work is considered to be the most definitive to the subject, I was/am inclined to believe him an egotist and "expert." I put the question: hadn't he gone just a little beyond the normal bounds of courtesy in his reply? My experience reveals this fact. Fortunately, or unfortunately, I made a significant contact. But my thinking to any good fortune would soon prove out false. Answering simple inquiry to the manumission of a "Prince Hall" in 1770 should have proved of little trouble and no difficulty. Instead my two letters met stony silence. No reply! No reply!

*Writer's Note:* That there is no public or private agency to supply information relative to the manumission of slaves in Massachusetts has been substantiated by the following:

1) Massachusetts Historical Society
2) Secretary of the Commonwealth.

Under date of 16 September 1963, the Boston Public Library informed, in part, the following:

> As to the first part of your inquiry, regarding the freeing of slaves in Massachusetts, I feel certain that we should be able to supply you with information. Your inquiry seems to denote that you wish some particular reference or event concerned with this matter. If you would give us more information as to just what intelligence you wish, I shall be glad to assist you further in this matter.

In Communication of 27 September, I requested specific information from the Boston Public Library on the manumission of a Prince

Hall in 1770. In reply of the Boston Public Library, under date of 10 October, it was indicated or can be deduced that they had communicated with Sherman in order to supply me information per my request. This disturbed me beyond reason. *The privacy of my request was lost.* Sherman was alerted. Isn't the Boston Public Library, as a city agency, supported by public funds? I was upset with the revealing and wanted to carry the matter a step or two further. No additional correspondence since this incident.

In April of 1964, I visited Boston, and in particular the Boston Anthenaeum. With the help of two reference librarians, I was able to locate a copy of a manumission certificate of a "Prince Hall," within the confines of the Price Notarial Records. You will understand that it was not an original document, for the diary purpose of Ezekiel Price or just for his personal records (non-official). This was the so-called certificate represented in the *"Philalethes Magazine"* (whole page 8½ x 11.) I have not seen the *original* nor do I believe Sherman has either. No doubt most readers will believe it to be an original. *Somehow* Sherman forgot to indicate it was just a copy or a record of a record.

*Writer's Note:* It is my thinking that Ezekiel Price no doubt kept and retained records of all transactions which came before him and so they have served to form the collection known as the Price Nortarial Records.

At this point I requested to be furnished a reproduction of the original memorial. I was informed that "Mr. Sherman, would gladly furnish me one of his copies." The librarians had both his home (he lives in Waltham 12 miles from Boston) and office phone numbers. It would be no trouble to contact him. With patience and some understanding I firmly informed them that I was not interested in any aid which Sherman could possibly supply. The message appeared to get over.

The problem now was how to procure reproduction without injury to the original. You will here understand that the memorial could not stand the natural light of day or ordinary lighting. In order for us to examine said item, it was necessary to remove same from any direct lighting to the shadows. To subject the memorial again to any new reproduction risked injury. It was decided to use the negative which was obtained with Sherman's original print. Upon search it was found missing. Sherman was the last one to have access to it. Opinion was passed: "he was too nice a man to have removed it." "he knew it would be quite difficult to obtain another;" "why would he do this?" "we have done many favors for him."

The fact remained that the item was missing, and Sherman was the last known individual to have had access to same. *Draw your own conclusions.*

It was then agreed to have another costly copy made up within ten days (I stressed the time element—it was agreed). I was asked if I would care to dictate certification so that same would be tailored to my needs. My dictation was taken and read for accuracy; I was satisfied. About three months later I received what appeared to be a positive print of the memorial in question from a S.M. Taylor Co. No indication that it was taken from the Price Notarial Records; no certification. The item was useless to me...

11. "Let not the 12 million Negroes be ashamed of the fact that they are the grand children of the slaves. There is no dishonour in being slaves. There is dishonour in being slave owners. But let us not think of honour and dishonour in connection with the past. Let us realize that the future is with those who would be truthful, pure and loving. For, as the old wise men have said, "truth ever is, untruth never was." Love alone binds and truth and love accrue only to the truly humble." *The Correspondence of W.E.B. DuBois, Vol. 1*, Edited by Herbert Aptheker (University of Massachusetts Press, 1973) p. 402

12. The following from the pen of Jacob Norton and printed in Appendix A—1873 Proceedings of the Prince Hall Grand Lodge of Massachusetts is of some interest:

> I now come to the American *Landmarks of Landmarks*, which, when abolished by the Grand Lodge of England in 1845, brought forth such a torrent of invective from our jurisprudence landmark sticklers—I mean the law of "freeborn." Assuming, now, for the sake of argument, that King Athelstan gave the indentical fifteen articles and fifteen points in Halliwell's MS. to the Masons in 926, and that those articles and points must forever be rewarded by Masons as equal to those recorded in Holy Writ, the question will then be, whether the compound word of "freeborn" can be found in Halliwell's MS.? *To this I answer in the negative.* The poem merely says, "That he no bondman prentys make."

Two reasons are assigned for that law. The first reason is, because the owner of the bondman was entitled to take his bondman away wherever he found him; and he might even take him out of the Lodge; and in that case the brethren might feel disposed to take sides with the unfortunate bondman, and would thus be brought into collision with the law of the land.

The second reason is based on the fable of the "Lord's children" that Euclid organized into the original fraternity. This, however, is too fanciful and frivolous to deserve notice. In Matthew Cooke's MS., written about a century after that of Halliwell, I find the phrase altered thus: "That no master, for no profit, take no apprentice for to be learned this is born of bond blood." For which law, he gives substantially the same reasons as Halliwell (the) MS. To make this perfectly clear, I herewith give the whole paragraph from Matthew Cooke's MS.

> That no master, for no profit, take no apprentice, for to be learned, that is born of bond blood, for because his Lord, to whom he is bound, will take him as well he may from his heart and lead him with him out of the Lodge, or out of his place that he worketh; for his fellows peradventure, would help him, and debate for him, and thereof manslaughter might arise—it is forbidden.

Putting aside the second reason as worthless, it is evident that the main reason is not applicable to being born in bondage, but merely to the *condition of being in bondage at the period of his apprenticeship.* And as the author of Cooke's MS. furnishes no reason why he changed the phraseologym and admitting the theory of "irremovable Landmarks," he had no right to change the phrase under any circumstances.

By substituting, therefore, the word "freeman" for "freeborn," the Grand Lodge of England very properly restored the legitimate Ancient Landmark, instead of removing one. "...being puzzled about the origin and reasons of the law of Freeborn," instead of seeking for information in the old Masonic MSS., they rushed to Cruden's *Concordance,* and finding there a reference to a passage, namely, "Send away the bondwoman and her son," they exclaimed. "Aha, here we have it, *freeborn,* is certainly a Masonic Landmark, because Grand Master Abraham was commended to send away the bondwoman," etc.

13. Wesley, *op cit.*, pp. 71-72.

14. *Ibid*, p. 51.

15. Davis, *op cit.*, p. 29.

16. The most definitive book on this period is Judge A. Leon Higginbotham, Jr., *In The Matter of Color* (New York, Oxford University Press, 1978)

17. "Black history records that the Blacks of the New World were *IN* but not *OF* Colonial America. They were the colonial subjects of the

colonial subjects of England. They were not being exploited by George III but by George Washington, Freemason and slaveowner, and his class. The White founding fathers were not the Black founding fathers, for the Black man lived a different Declaration of Independence, a different Revolution and a different America. Lerone Bennett, Jr. is correct in *The Shaping of Black America* when he writes:

> The idea is simple, but the implications are profound and require a rethinking of the time-line of Black America, which began with the black pioneers and not the white founding fathers. The white founding fathers were not the black founding fathers; the white constitutional convention was not the black constitutional convention; the white beginning was not the black beginning.

*The Phylaxis Magazine,* comments on John Sherman's Review of Life and Legacy, Part IV by Joseph A. Walkes, Jr. There are and have always been two Americas, one White and one Black. To define them together is impossible. To measure the Freemasonry of each together is likewise impossible.

18. One of the great works on Prince Hall Freemasonry is *Masonry Among Colored Men in Massachusetts* by P.G.M. Lewis Hayden (1871). In referring to "The antimasonic dogma put forth by them (Massachusetts Grand Lodge) in the organization of their grand lodge is that of "assumption,"—of late, "revolution and assumption," as set up by G.M. Gardner, of Massachusetts, in an address before his Grand Lodge..."the origin of "assumption." These same brethren, after the demise of Joseph Warren, then carried their assumption still further, and organized themselves into what their assumption enabled them to call a Grand Lodge, *de jure,* which Brother Norton has set forth after the following style. To begin with, we first give the names of those who met, and shall show by what authority:

Jos. Webb, D.G.M., St. Andrew's Lodge, Boston
Paul Revere, S.G.M., St. Andrew's Lodge, Boston
Thomas Crafts, J.G.W., St. Andrew's Lodge, Boston
John Lowell, G. Treas., St. Andrew's Lodge, Boston
Nat. Pierece, G. Sec., St. Andrew's Lodge, Boston
Thomas Uran, S.G.D., St. Andrew's Lodge, Boston
Edward Proctor, J.G.D., St. Andrew's Lodge, Boston
Moses Deshon, P.M., of Tyrian Lodge, Gloucester
Philip Marrett, G. Stewards, St. Andrew's Lodge, Boston
Winthrop Grey, G. Stewards, St. Andrews's Lodge, Boston
William Greenough, M., St. Peter's Newburyport.

Of the illegality of their proceedings, Brother Norton speaks thus:

And be it further remembered, that the whole number of
Lodges under the provincialship of Joseph Warren was just
four, two of which were located in Boston; of one Boston
Lodge, viz., "Massachusetts Lodge," not a solitary member was
present in 1770. The S.W. of St. Andrew's Lodge attended by
virtue of his defunct commission of Grand Steward. St. Andrew's Lodge did not authorize him to represent her, because
she did not join the said G.L. until 1809. Moses Deshon was
neither master nor warden; hence the only legal representative
then present was the master of St. Peter's Lodge, Newburyport.
He represented a lodge; the rest represented only their individual selves. And this solitary master of a lodge, associated
with ten unauthorized brethren, assembled in an upper
chamber of a tavern, and there and then elected each other into
various kind of worshipfuls, and declared themselves the G.L.
of Masschusetts; while hundreds of masons and a number of
lodges then existing in the State, were neither represented nor
consulted.

We now ask, in the name of justice and common sense,
whether the action of such a body could be looked upon as bind-
ing upon all. Nay, we will go a little further, and suppose that
Brother Greenough was unauthorized by his lodge to attend the
said meeting. Who can deny that St. Peter's Lodge had not a
right to repudiate its master's unauthorized assumption? In that
case the new organization could claim to be a G.L. *only* over
the lodge they chartered on the day of their organization. The
rest of the brotherhood in the State retained their inherent
right, either to remain tributary to their parent G.L., to
organize a new one, or to join the one just organized.

Is this the standard by which American Grand Lodges are required to organize, that is, by individuals representing
themselves, as in this case? Or is it not, as given by Chase, thus:
"A certain number of Lodges, not less than *three*, holding
charters or warrants from some legal grand lodge, or from different grand lodges, meet in convention by their representatives, formally resolve to organize a grand lodge, adopt a constitution and proceed to elect and install their officers.

"It is necessary that it be separate State of Territory; that
there be no grand lodge at that time existing within it; that at

least three chartered lodges be, at the time, in active existence within the territorial limits, and consent to the formation of such Grand Lodge; that they meet in convention as *lodges*, and not as individuals; that they adopt a constitution; and that the newly elected Grand Master be installed by some P.G. Master, or by the senior past master present." It is upon this action of those eleven men that G.M. Gardner rests his case, as you will perceive by reference to his address, the refutation of which will force them to seek another subterfuge whereon to build.

As there are lessons in the great light of Freemasonry which are applicable to him and his lodge, commanding "that they enter in at the strait gate," we would call their attention to what follows: "Veryily, veryily, I say unto you, he that entereth not by the door into the sheepfold, but climbeth up some other way, the same is a thief and a robber." This is applicable to their case. Having "stolen into the sheepfolds," as beyond question they have, what have they done but endeavored to rob us of our masonic character? Verily, the next is full-filled. We say, by what authority? For in the organization of a grand lodge it is to be remembered that it must be the free act of the masons whose grand lodge it is to be; and since we have found that it was not a grand lodge of the masons of Massachusetts, but a grand lodge of eleven unauthorized men, as shown by their records, it should be repudiated by masons throughout the world.

Here now, are two bodies that make up the masonic history of the State. And if the above be true, which they cannot in truth deny, are they not to be commended for the dode of "revolution and assumption?" We would like to know to what other refuge they could have fled. Their masonry is a fraud, and therefore there could be no usage for their organization; for the reason that the laws, rules and regulations of masonry are to control the action of masons only, and none others. We repreat, "revolution and assumption" were indeed convenient. To these they escaped with the vain hope of hiding their deformity from the all piercing eye of Truth. Vain hope!

We shall show that the Massachusetts masons...cannot substitute their legitimate connection with the Grand Lodge of England...The first we learn of Massachusetts masons is not that they assembled at any place, to be initiated, passed and raised, as we have yet to learn of there having been any lodge convened prior to the one which assembled on the 30th of July, 1733 (it being the first lodge that assembled on the continent) at Boston, without authority from any source for any purpose whatever, so that the query now is, when and where did they receive their masonry? This Lodge did not assemble for the purpose, viz, that of *initiating, passing* and *raising,* but under the fallacious pretence that, to them, had been granted (through Henry Price) a charter to open a grand lodge, grant charters, etc.; not a word of which was true, as to this day, no appearance of the name of Henry Price, or his lodge of 1733, is to be found upon the records of the Grand Lodge of England."

It is this writer's contention that if the Grand Lodge of Massachusetts can claim "revolution and assumption" then so can Prince Hall Freemasonry.

19. "... the earliest published speech of Black American—Prince Hall's Masonic sermon of July 24, 1797" *The Voice of Black America: Major Speeches by Negroes in the United States, 1797-1971"* edited by Philip S. Foner. (New York, Simon and Schuster, 1972) p. 1. However, Bro. John Marrant, Chaplain of African Lodge No. 459 preached a sermon on June 24, 1789, See Walkes, *op cit.,* p. 24.

20. Wesley, *op cit.,* pp 208-219.

21. This comes from the statement from Rev. John Eliott, D.D., one of the founders of the Historical Society, and pastor of the New North Church, in Boston. The statement is from the *Belknap Papers,* 1795, p. 383.

There is much harmony between blacks and whites. We seldom have contentions, except in houses of ill-fame, where some very *depraved white* females get among the blacks. This has issued in the pulling down such houses at times, and caused several actions at Justices' Courts these two years past. Otherwise, they do not associate. Even religious societies, those not of public fellowship, are separate in the town of Boston. And, what is still *more remarkable, white and black masons* do not sit together in their lodges. The African Lodge in Boston, though possessing a charter from England, signed by the Earl of Effingham, and countersigned by the Duke of Cumberland, meet by themselves; and white masons, not more skilled in geometry than their black brethren, will not acknowledge them. The reason given is that the blacks were made clandestinely in the first place, which, being known, would have prevented them from receiving a charter. But this enquiry would not have been made about *white lodges*, many of which have not conformed to the rules of *Masonry*. The truth is, they are ashamed of being *on an equality with blacks*. Even the fraternal kiss of France, given to *merit*, without distinction in colour, doth not influence Massachusetts masons to give an embrace less emphatical, or tender and affectionate to their *black brethren*. These, on the other hand, valuing themselves upon their knowledge of the craft, think themselves better masons in other respects than the *whites*, because *Masonry* considers all men *equal who are free;* and Massachusetts laws admit of no kind of slavery. It is evident from this that neither *"avowedly nor tacitly"* do the blacks admit the preeminence of the *whites;* but as evidence that the preeminence is claimed by the *whites*.

This statement is again produced in a letter from Dr. Belknap to St. George Tucker in Virginia, who raised a number of questions respecting slavery. In Dr. Wesley's *Prince Hall* the actual statement as written by Belknap is reproduced on page 52-53. It is however, interesting to note that in John Sherman's review of Dr. Wesley's book in the *Transactions of Quatuor Coronati* Vol. 90, p. 307, Sherman deliberately does not give the full quote.

William H. Upton: The Prince Hall's Letter Book, *Transactions of Quatuor Coronati*, Vol. 13, p. 56 reads:

> Dear Brother, I would inform you that this Lodge hath been founded almost eight years and we have had only a Permit to Walk on St. Johns Day and to Bury our Dead in manner and form. We have had no opportunity to apply for a Warrant before now, though we have been importuned to send to France for one, yet we thought it best to send to the Fountain from whence we received the Light, for a Warrant; and now Dear Br. we must make you our advocate at the Grand Lodge, hoping you will be so good (in our name and Stead) to lay this Before the Royal Grand Master and the Grand Wardens and the rest of the Grand Lodge, who we hope will not deny us nor treat us Beneath the rest of our fellowmen, although Poor yet Sincere Brethren of the Craft.

It is interesting to note, that Upton made it clear that the material that makes up the letter book is handwritten by Prince Hall:

> As a rule it is quite legible; on a number of pages the ink is nearly bleached out, while on others it is as black as when first

written. The spelling is often phonetic, the capitalization that of the last century; and of punctuation or paragraphing there is practically none. I have seen no advantge in retaining these peculiarities in the extracts quoted below, save in a few instance.

However, Sherman in his review of Dr. Wesley's book amplified Hall's errors by quoting a portion of the above letter:

Dear Dr. I would inform you that this lodge hath Bin Founded almost this Eight yeears and had no Warrant yet by only a Premete (sic) From Grand Master Row (Rowe) to walk on St. Johnn's Dayes and to Burey our Dead in forme; which we now Injoy: We have had no opportunity *tell* now of aplieing for a Warrant,-

22. George Draffen of Newington, (*Transactions of Quatuor Coronati Lodge*, Vol. 89) p. 75.

The petition was successful and the Grand Lodge of England (moderns) issued a warrant to African Lodge No. 459 on 20 September 1784. For a number of reasons did not arrive in Boston until April 1787. Its arrival was announced in the *Columbian Sentinel*, a Boston newspaper dated 2 May 1787, in the following words: "By Captain Scott, from London, came the charter, etc." According to Grimshaw, the lodge was erected on 6 May 1787, but we are left in the dark as to the manner of its erection and by whom it was carried out. Prince Hall also received a copy of the Constitutions of the Grand Lodge and they contained a requirement that each lodge must be properly constituted. To what extent that requirement was observed by lodges overseas is open to doubt; if there was another lodge in the area or near at hand there would be little difficulty in complying with the rules. If it was an isolated lodge, strict compliance may have been impossible.

The reverence that modern Prince Hall Freemasonry pays to this document can be seen as recorded by the Prince Hall Masonic Research Society, the Phylaxis Society, which was holding its annual meeting in Boston in 1978, and viewed the Warrant. Joseph A. Walkes, Jr., *Ibid*, p. 156.

23. William H. Upton: *Negro Masonry, being a Critical Examination of objections to the legitimacy of the Masonry existing among the Negroes of America*, (Massachusetts, M.W.P.H.G.L. of Mass., 1902) p. 210.

24. *The Prince Hall Cousellor:* a manual of guidance designed to aid those combating clandestine Freemasonry (Prince Hall Grand Masters' Conference, 1965) between pages 40 and 41.

25. *The Phylaxis,* Vol. VI, No. 1, 1st Quarter, 1980, page 10. Comments on John Sherman's Review of *Life and Legacy.* The feelings and beliefs of Prince Hall Freemasonry must be understood. Be they right or wrong, the fact remains, that they are what is accepted by the Prince Hall Craft, and it is doubtful that they ever will be changed.

26. John E. "Bruce-Grit" Bruce, well-known Black Journalist, wrote that Prince Hall "was employed as a steward on one of the many vessels plying between Boston and England, and that the African Lodge evolved from a little club in Boston." sce Walkes: *op cit.,* p. 3. Also see footnote No. 3 above.

27. Newington: *op cit.,* p. 77. ...African Lodge was still writing to London in its capacity as a private lodge under the Grand Lodge of England (Moderns) and sending in returns and fees. Lane records that the last payment of fees was made in 1797. On 15 June 1802 Prince Hall wrote yet again to Grand Secretary White and said, *inter alia:*

> I have sent a number of letters to the Grand Lodge and money for the Grand Charity, and by faithful brethren as I thought, but I have not received one letter from the Grand Lodge for the five years, which I thought somewhat strange at first; but when I heard so many were taken by the French, I thought otherwise, and prudent not to send.

*Prince Hall's Letter Book* contains a copy of yet a further letter, of 16 August 1806, to William White complaining that he had not received any answers to his letters since 1792. From that it is clear that Prince Hall and African Lodge were still of the view that, as late as in 1806, African Lodge was still a private Lodge under the Grand Lodge of England. William White seems either to have neglected to answer Prince Hall's letters—or possibly never to have received them. In this latter respect one can hardly suppose that all Prince Hall's letters failed to reach their destination.

28. Bro. Samuel Evan's report of the petition of Grand Master Lewis Hayden of the Prince Hall Grand Lodge of Massachusetts to the Caucasian Grand Lodge of Massachusetts must be read. The entire article as written by Bro. Evans appears in *The Phylaxis,* Vol. V., No. 3-4th Quarter, 1979, pages 43-44.

29. Sherman's *Review of Life and Legacy, op cit.*, p. 308. One of the entries shows a date of 1781, which shows that the entire table had to have been written after that date.

30.    My Dear Bro. Caldwell,—I informed you some time ago of having seen an African Lodge record, covering the period of its alleged dormancy. I will now say something more. The record begins in 1807. The first minutes mentions the raising of Era Lew, and between the above date and 1826 near eighty members were initiated. The party who gave me the record imagined that was an *original* record; but, on running hastily over a few of its pages, I noticed that while names of the secretaries were changed, the penmanship was the same. This made me turn to what may be called title-page of the book, where I found the following: "The Book of Records of the Grand African Lodge, No. 459, Boston, November 25, A.L. 5825.' This entry confirmed my suspicion of the record being a mere transcript. Pursuing my examination, I came to November 21, 1825, where I found a motion to purchase a book in order to transcribe the records, and three dollars was given to Hilton to buy a book, and he was autorized to transcribe it. June 15, 1826, a motion was made to pay Hilton for transcribing the record, and there the transcript ends. From that date to 1846 the minutes are all original. Each secretary shows a distinct kind of penmanship. I have not a shadow of a doubt that the transcript was copied from the then existing record. The internal evidence to that effect would satisfy any impartial tribunal.

Grand Lodge of Ohio: *Report of Committee on Foreign Communications, 1876*, by John D. Caldwell, Chairman, p. 117-118.

31. This writer, besides having the microfilm of the minutes of African Lodge, also has a complete photocopy of same. One section reads:

*BOSTON, November 7th, 1807*

Prince Hall, Grand Master Deceas'd

Prince Hall was quite alive on that date, having died December 4th. There are also a number of areas that raise some questions: for instance, on the same cover sheet, John Shorter is listed as the Secretary December 28th, 1807, but the minutes of June 4, 1808 states "that he should be raised on the first Tuesday of November by paying down two dollars." It also says that "John Shorter was rais'd to the *Sublime Degree* of Master Mason."

However, if we are to trust Mackey on this one instance, his *Revised Encyclopedia of Freemasonry*, Volume 2, pg. 983 "the first book in which we meet the adjective *sublime* applied to the Third Degree, is the Masonic Discourses of Dr. T.M. Harris, published at Boston in 1801. Cole also used it in 1817..."

It would seem to this writer that the use of the entire words, "raised to the Sublime Degree of Master Mason" was not in practice until after 1817.

This writer has photocopies written on long legal size pages, and photocopies written on short pages, and they add to the mystery. The long legal size pages appear to be a transcript of the short pages, but they do not agree. For instance, one shows a meeting held November 8th, 1808 while the other shows a meeting held November 9th. One also shows a meeting being held November 10th while the other shows no meeting for that date.

The meeting held June 14th, 1808 is a case in point. One reads: Boston, June 14th, 1808:

> St. Johns day agreed upon by a committee chosen by the Lodge that John Cooper, John Shorter and Walter Martens to pay out of the fund for the use of the Hall the sum for Lodge expences eight dollars _____ *$8.00.*

The other reads:

Boston, June 14th 1808:

> Chose John Cooper, John Shorter and Walter Marten a committee to pay out of the fund Eight dollars for the use of the room.

Without a doubt we are dealing with two different records, one at least being a transcript of another. However, both records could be a transcript, and copied in case one became lost.

**As stated in the text, it is very clear to this writer that the re-written minutes of African Lodge cannot be used as the basis of Masonic research.**

32. The following from Jacob Norton to John D. Caldwell is of some interest:

> Last week I was informed that Thomas Dalton, who according to the record, was initiated in the African Lodge April 11, 1825, lived in Charlestown, now part of Boston. The said Dalton is eighty-three years of age. He owns a brick house in Boston, a wooden house in Charlestown, and a farm in New

Hampshire, and he occasionally resides for a few months in each place. Well, *I interviewed him.* I took with me a list of the names of the Africans made in the African Lodge from 1808 to 1826, and I read the roll to him. The first on the roll was Era Lew. "Oh!" said he, "he was a relative of mine. There were two other brothers who were Masons." In short, twenty-three on the list he knew to be Masons before he was made one. Three on the list he remembered, but did not recollect that he heard of their being Masons. They left the lodge before he joined it. About thirty-five on the list he had no recollection of. *Remember*, these were all made before he joined the Lodge. When I came to Wm. Brown, Wm. Kerr, Walker Lewis, etc., "Oh!" said he, "they were made the same night I was." And so they were.

I asked him whether he had heard, either before his initiation or after his initiation, from any of the old members of the African Lodge having ceased to meet at any time between 1807 and 1824. He said his earliest recollection of the Lodge was a funeral of one of its members, he believed about 1810. Next, he said, the three brothers Lew and one Howard were musicians. They were then the fashionable musicians for private parties among the Boston aristocracy. He, he said, always used to be engaged at those parties as a waiter, and he distinctly recollects that many times conversations took place among the above named parties in his presence about the African Lodge. Besides, he said, "I knew Moddy well, and spent a good deal of time in his company some years before I was made a Mason, and then I frequently heard allusions made to the lodge." He furthermore said, "I have never heard of the alleged dormacy of the Lodge before you told me that such reports were printed in Masonic proceedings." "Besides," he added, "I was keeper of the Lodge archives, and, to the best of my recollection, we had records covering the whole period of its alleged dormancy. The statement of its dormancy is, therefore, false."

The same statement he repeated to Bro. Pulisifer, a highly respected brother, member of the Winslow Lewis Lodge. The next thing I did was, I drew up a paper, and induced Dalton to swear to it before a justice of the peace. Pulsifer, who is clerk in the Secretary of State office, copied it, to which Dalton's signature was attached and sworn to, and the said affidavit will be printed in one of the Boston papers in a few days... (page 118-119)

The Dalton affidavit is listed on page 43 of Harry E. Davis' book.

I must say, that I cannot imagine Caucasians coming into the Black community to see if African Lodge was meeting or not. On the other hand, our Caucasian counterparts do not have much room to talk. If we accept the Hon. Josiah H. Drummond P.G.M. of Maine, "*Historical and Bibliographical Memoranda:*

> *Alabama*—organized in June 1821, and met again in December following. It did not meet in 1832...nor in 1835 when it suspended labor. It was reorganized in December 1836.
>
> *Arkansas*—organized in 1806. No proceedings from 1807 to 1824, 1831 to 1844 and 1846 to 1849.
>
> *District of Columbia*—organized in 1811. No proceedings from 1827 to 1844.
>
> *Illinois*—It died in 1827 or possibly in 1828, reorganized in 1840.
>
> *Louisiana*—No session in 1832. No proceedings from 1834 to 1840.
>
> *Maryland*—organized in 1783. Reorganized in 1787.
>
> *Massachusetts*—First proceedings, according to Drummond, printed in 1803.
>
> *Michigan*—Organized in 1826. Suspended labor in 1829. In 1841 it met and reorganized.
>
> *New York*—which is quite confusing to say the least, as it formed with other Grand Lodges, St. John's and Phillips Grand Lodge, and then into city and country Grand Lodges. In any case, the city Grand Lodge published no proceedings in 1823 to 1826, and the country Grand Lodge did not publish in 1823 to 1826.
>
> *North Carolina*—first organized in 1771, suspended, re-organized in 1787.
>
> *South Carolina*—organized in 1754, and like New Yok had some problems. However the proceedings for 1817 were not published.
>
> *Tennessee*—organized in 1813. It did not meet in 1861 or 1862.
>
> *Vermont*—organized in 1794. Suspended in 1836, and reorganized.
>
> *Virginia*—no session in 1838.
>
> *Wisconsin*—no annual session in 1844 or 1851.

33. The following article by Harry A. Williamson may be of some interest:

> The charge has been made frequently that African Lodge No. 459, was without any authority to establish other Lodges and to prove the falsity of that charge due to the fact that such was the custom of the period, the following data concerning two Lodges are cited.
>
> One of these is "Mother" Kilwinning at Kilwinning, Scotland, erected in 1599, and the other is Lodge Melrose St. John, No. 1 at Newstead, later at Melrose. "Mother" Kilwinning has no number but is designated with the letter "O" of the alphabet.
>
> The iist of lodges erected by "Mother" Kilwinning both before and after the formation of the Grand Lodge of Scotland as recorded in "Scottish Masonic Records" compiled by the Very Worshipful Grand Librarian of the Grand Lodge of Scotland and published in 1950 is as follows:

1. Airdrie Kilwinning—charterd December 20, 1749.
2. Beith Kilwinning—chartered December 26, 1754.
3. Bathgate Kilwinning—chartered December 21, 1784.
4. Canongate Kilwinning—chartered December 20, 1677.(*)
5. Cumberland Kilwinning—chartered February 4, 1747.
6. Cessnock Kilwinning—chartered January 21, 1748.
7. Doric Port Glascow Kilwinning—chartered January 24, 1759.
8. Duns Kilwinning—chartered before 1736.(*)
9. East Kilbridge Kilwinning—chartered February 8, 1738.(#)
10. Reskine Kilwinning—chartered July 28, 1770.
11. Fort George Kilwinning—chartered June 24, 1756.
12. Falmouth Kilwinning (Virginia)—chartered December 20, 1775.
13. High Knight Templar of Ireland Kilwinning—chartered October 8, 1779.
14. Hamilton Kilwinning—chartered before 1770.
15. Largs Kilwinning—chartered December 1, 1767.
16. Lennox Kilwinning—chartered June 24, 1772.
17. Leith Kilwinning—chartered before 1736. (*)
18. Mountstewart—chartered December 21, 1768.
19. Montgomerie Cunningham East Kilbridge Kilwinning—chartered October 6, 1803.
20. Montgomerie Kilwinning—chartered December 10, 1800.

21. Moortown of Carron Kilwinning—chartered April 8, 1734 (*)
22. Old Kilwinnng St. John—chartered in 1678. (*)
23. Paisley Kilwinning—chartered August 5, 1749.
24. Provan Kilwinning—chartered December 3, 1754.
25. Patrick Kilwinning—chartered May 24, 1759.
26. Pythagorian—chartered October 1, 1767.
27. Paisley St. Morrin—chartered before 1772.
28. Renfrew County Kilwinning—chartered February 12, 1755.
29. Riccarton Kilwinning—chartered November 1, 1768.
30. Squaremen's Ayr Kilwinning—chartered September 9, 1765.
31. Stranraer Kilwinning—chartered February 22, 1768.
32. St. Bryde's—chartered May 2, 1769.
33. St. John—chartered November 14, 1734 (*)
34. St. Andrew—chartered December 21, 1791.
35. St. John Kilwinning Kirk of Glascow St. Mungo Lodge—
    chartered between 1728 and 1729. (*)
36. Scotts Greys Kilwinning—chartered in 1747.
37. St. Andrews (Glasgow Journeymen Free Operatives)—chartered in
    1741.
38. Sanquhar Kilwinning—chartered May 11, 1738.
39. St. Andrew—chartered before 1802.
40. St. David—chartered June 5, 1758.
41. Torphichen Kilwinning—chartered May 15, 1729. (*)
42. Tappahannock (Essex County Virginia)—chartered June 3, 1758.
43. Tarbolton St. James—chartered May 17, 1771.
44. Wigtown Kilwinning—chartered December 20, 1755.
45. Lodge of Glascow St. Mungo—chartered 1728. (*)
46. Loudon Kilwinning—chartered March 14, 1741.
47. Dumfries Kilwinning—chartered May 20, 1687.(*)

The above record reveals that "Mother" Kilwinning established 7 lodges prior to her entry into the Grand Lodge of Scotland(*); that, in all probability she erected another (#) while she was still in that Grand Lodge, and 36 after she had left the Grand Lodge in 1743 and her return in 1808.

The following are the Lodges which were erected by Lodge Melrose St. John:

(a) Glascow Melrose St. John—chartered October 26, 1872.
(b) Melrose St. Mungo—chartered June 28, 1873.
(c) Greenock No. 3 (†)
(d) Lenzie No. 4 (†)
(e) Shettleston No. 5 (†)

(†) concerning these Lodges the records says their existence was known but dates and names are unknown.

It is to be noted that Kilwinning Glascow was a "self-constituted" Lodge from April 1, 1735, until its Charter was confirmed by the Grand Lodge in October 27, 1737.

Lodge of Glascow St. John No. 3 bis, was an *independent* body from its inception in 1628 until it joined the Grand Lodge May 6, 1850

It does seem to this writer that African Lodge No. 459 pales when compared to the above record.

34. Prince Hall died December 4, 1807, and the notice of death and funeral was published in six Boston newspapers. They agree that his age was 72 years, that he was Master of African Lodge, and that a Masonic ceremony was held. Sherman and others make a point to add that the death notices do not tell where the remains were interred, nor can this be found in the official city records. The grave of a former wife, Sarah Ritchey, who died February 26, 1769, is located in the Copp's Hill burying ground, and on the back side of this stone, the following epitaph to Prince Hall was added, evidently many years after he died.

"Here lies ye body of
Prince Hall
First Grand Master of the
Colored Grand Lodge of
Masons in Mass.

Died Dec. 7, 1807"

Walkes: *op cit*, p. 7

35. John M. Sherman, "More About Prince Hall: Notes and Documents" *The Philalethes*, June 1962, page 42 and 45.

36. William Copp, "a gentleman of color" who owned considerable land in that area and in all probability that comprising the cemetery. *The Phylaxis Magazine*, Vol. VIII. No. 2, 2nd Quarter, 1982, page 30. .

# PART TWO

# The Formation of the Prince Hall Grand Lodges

1. **Is it true that mainstream Grand Lodges have adhered to State lines as the limits of their activities, and only one Grand Lodge can operate in any State in the United States?**

   The concept sounds good on paper, but in truth there has never been such a thing in the United States. For more than one hundred years two Masonic powers, one mainstream (in the White community) the other, Prince Hall in the Black, have existed. It is, and has always been true. Any person who believes otherwise is not in the least familiar with the history, traditions, and the procedures of Freemasonry as it prevails in many places.[1]

2. **What was the title and date of formation of the first Black Grand Lodge?**

   Tradition has it that it was **African Grand Lodge of North America,** organized in Boston, Massachusetts; June 24, 1791 with the following officers:

   Prince Hall, Grand Master
   Cyrus Forbs, Senior Grand Warden
   George Middleton, Junior Grand Warden
   Peter Best, Grand Treasurer
   Prince Taylor, Grand Secretary

   Like its Caucasian counterpart, the Grand Lodge of Massachusetts, which claims it is the first Grand Lodge in the Western Hemisphere,[2] the Prince Hall Grand Lodge records show that the first mention of a Grand Lodge was recorded June 15, 1827, *viz* "This evening the grand african lodge 459 met for special business." However, as mentioned earlier, there is much confusion concerning the early minutes.[3]

3. **What was the title, date and location of the second Grand Lodge of Blacks?**

Tradition has it as **African Lodge No. 459 of Philadelphia,** June 24, 1797 and its officers were:

Rev. Absalom Jones, Master
James Forten, Senior Warden
William Harding, Junior Warden
Jonathan Harding, Treasurer
Peter Richmond, Secretary
R. Venable, Senior Deacon
John Davis, Junior Deacon[4]

4. **What was the third grand body?**

"Boyer Grand Lodge F. & A.M.," March 12, 1845 in New York City, Title changed to "United Grand Lodge, F. & A.M." at its re-organization in 1848. Formed a union with a rival body in the state on December 27, 1878 and became "Grand Lodge, F. & A.M. of the State of New York." In 1919, added as a suffix the phrase "Prince Hall." Its present title is **Most Worshipful Prince Hall Grand Lodge of the Most Ancient and Honorable Fraternity of Free and Accepted Masons of the State of New York,** which was adopted in June 1944 at its annual session. Location of its Grand East is 454 West 155th Street, New York City, New York 10032. Annual Communication is held the first Wednesday in June, and as of 1980 it has approximately 77 lodges, and total membership of 8,506.

5. **Fourth?**

"African Grand Lodge of Maryland" organized in 1845 (exact date unknown to this writer), at Baltimore. The title was later changed to "United Grand Lodge," but is now known as **The Most Worshipful Prince Hall Grand Lodge**

F. & A.M. State of Maryland and Jurisdiction. Location of its Grand East is 1307 Eutaw Place, Baltimore, Maryland 21217. Annual Communication is held second Sunday in August, and as of 1980 it had 91 lodges with a total membership of 6,000.

6.  **Fifth?**

"Union Grand Lodge" formed in the District of Columbia March 27, 1848. It is now known as **The Most Worshipful Prince Hall Grand Lodge, Free and Accepted Masons, PHA, District of Columbia Incorporated.** Location of its Grand East is 1000 You Street, N.W., Washington, D.C. 20001. Annual communication is the second Wednesday in December. Number of lodges 23, total membership 5,799.

7.  **Sixth?**

Erected June 24, 1848 in the city of Trenton and is titled **Most Worshipful Prince Hall Grand Lodge F. & A.M. State of New Jersey.** Its Grand East is located at 188-190 Irvine Turner Boulevard, Newark, New Jersey 07108. Number of lodges 52, total membership 5,491.

8.  **Seventh?**

Organized at Cincinnati, May 3, 1849, title is **The Most Worshipful Prince Hall Grand Lodge of Ohio F. & A.M.** Location of its Grand East is 50 Hamilton Park, Columbus, Ohio 43203. Number of lodges 66, total membership 7,248.

9.  **Eighth?**

Erected June 9, 1849 in Wilmington as "Hiram Grand Lodge" and changed its title in 1944 to **The Most Worshipful Prince Hall Grand Lodge F. & A.M. of Delaware.** Location of its Grand East is 623 South Heald Street, Wilmington, Delaware 19801. Annual communication is held fourth Friday in June. Number of lodges 16, total membership 930.

10. **Ninth?**

Founded June 19, 1855 in San Francisco as "Grand Lodge, Free, Ancient and Accepted York Masons." Its title is now,

**Most Worshipful Prince Hall Grand Lodge F. & A.M. State of California Incorporated.** Location of its Grand East is Post Office Box 8, Vallejo, California 94590. Number of lodges 92, total membership 7,500.

## 11. Tenth?

September 13, 1856 was formed in Indianapolis as **The Most Worshipful Prince Hall Grand Lodge, F. & A.M. Jurisdiction of Indiana.** Location of its Grand East is 653 Northwest Street, Indianapolis, Indiana 46202. Annual communication is the first Friday in August; total membership 3,043.

## 12. Eleventh?

Founded as "Harmony Grand Lodge, F. & A.M. of Rhode Island and Providence Plantations" October 7, 1858. It is now **Most Worshipful Prince Hall Grand Lodge F. & A.M. of the State of Rhode Island.** Location of Grand East is 883 Eddy Street, Providence, Rhode Island 02905. Annual commnication is the second Saturday in June, total number of lodges 5, membership 450.

## 13. Twelfth?

"Eureka Grand Lodge" was founded in New Orleans January 5, 1863. Formed a union with a National Compact Grand Lodge in 1878, but maintained its name. Known to-day as **Most Worshipful Prince Hall Grand Lodge F. & A.M. for the State of Louisiana and Jurisdiction.** Location of its Grand East is 1335-37 North Boulevard, Baton Rouge, Louisiana 70821. Annual communication Tuesday preceding St. John the Baptist Day. Number of lodges 174, total membership 10,299.

## 14. Thirteenth?

"Union Grand Lodge" formed at Niles, April 25, 1866. It is now titled **The Most Worshipful Prince Hall Grand Lodge F. & A.M. of Michigan.** Location of Grand East is 3100

Gratiot Avenue, Detroit, Michigan 48207. Annual communication Monday preceding fourth Tuesday in April. Number of lodges 48, total membership 6,000.

### 15. Fourteenth?

Founded October 29, 1865 as "Grand Lodge A.F. & A.M. (Prince Hall Affiliation)." Today known as **Most Worshipful Prince Hall Grand Lodge of Virginia F. & A.M., Incorporated.** Location of its Grand East is 1800 Monsview Place, Lynchburg, Virginia 24504. Annual communication is third Tuesday in September. Number of lodges 226, total membership 15,172.

### 16. Fifteenth?

"Grand Lodge, F. & A.M. of Kentucky" established in Louisville, August 16, 1866. It is now **Most Worshipful Prince Hall Grand Lodge F. & A.M. of Kentucky.** Location of its Grand East is 215 East Walnut Street, Midway, Kentucky 40347. Annual communication is the first Tuesday in August. Number of lodges 82, total membership 3,500.

### 17. Sixteenth?

Established in St. Louis, December 20, 1866 as "Grand Lodge Free and Accepted Ancient York Masons for the State of Missouri." It is now **The Most Worshipful Prince Hall Grand Lodge, F. & A.M. of Missouri and Jurisdiction.** Location of its Grand East is 4525 Olive Street, St. Louis, Missouri 63108. Annual communication is second Wednesday in July. Number of lodges 65, total membership 3,715 of which this writer is one.

### 18. Seventeenth?

"Grand Lodge, Free and Accepted Ancient York Masons" organized at Springfield, February 15, 1867. Known today as **Most Worshipful Prince Hall Grand Lodge F. & A.M. State of Illinois.** Location of its Grand East is 809 East 42nd Place, Chicago, Illinois 60653. Annual communication is held second Tuesday in October. Number of lodges 81, total membership 6,500.

### 19. Eighteenth?

Erected at Charleston in June 1867, it is known as **Most Worshipful Prince Hall Grand Lodge of F. & A.M. of the State of South Carolina.** Location of its Grand East is 2324 Gervais Street, Columbia, South Carolina 29204. Annual communication is second Monday in December. Number of lodges 316, total membership 19,193.

### 20. Nineteenth?

"King Solomon Grand Lodge" September 11, 1867, now known as **Most Worshipful Prince Hall Grand Lodge F. & A.M. of Kansas and its Jurisdiction.** Location of its Grand East is P.O. Box 1117, Kansas City, Kansas 66117. Annual communication is the first week in June. Number of lodges 48, total membership 2,534.

### 21. Twentieth?

Erected in the City of Wilmington, March 1, 1870 as the "Grand Lodge of Free and Accepted Ancient York Masons," known today as **Most Worshipful Prince Hall Grand Lodge F. & A.M., Jurisdiction of North Carolina.** Location of its Grand East is 1405 East Washington Street, Greensboro, North Carolina 27420. Annual communication is first Tuesday in October. Number of lodges 326, total membership 20,050.

### 22. Twenty-first?

Title is "Union Grand Lodge F. & A.M. of Florida" founded in Jacksonville, June 17, 1870. Known today as **Most Worshipful Union Grand Lodge Most Ancient and Honorable Fraternity F. & A.M., P.H.A., Florida & Belize, Central America Jurisdiction, Inc.** Location of its Grand East is 410 Broad Street, Jacksonville, Florida 32202. Annual communication is fourth Tuesday in April. Number of lodges 209, total membership is 9,500.

### 23. Twenty-second?

"Union Grand Lodge, A.F. & A.M. Of Georgia" established in Savannah, August 22, 1870. Known today as **Most Worshipful Prince Hall Grand Lodge F. & A.M., Jurisdiction of Georgia.** Location of its Grand East is 330 Auburn Avenue, N.E., Atlanta, Georgia 30335. Annual communication, second Tuesday in June. Number of lodges 205, total membership 20,000.

### 24. Twenty-third?

**Prince Hall Grand Lodge, F. & A.M. of Tennessee,** was established at Nashville, August 31, 1870. Location of its Grand East is 253 South Parkway, West, Memphis, Tennessee 38109. Annual communication, first Monday in August. Number of lodges 201, total membership 8,000.

### 25. Twenty-fourth?

Erected in the City of Mobile, as "Grand Lodge A.F. & A.M." and is now known as **Most Worshipful Prince Hall Grand Lodge F. & A.M. of Alabama.** Location of its Grand East is 1630 North 4th Avenue, Birmingham, Alabama 35203. Annual communication third Tuesday in July. Number of lodges 541, total membership 20,450.

### 26. Twenty-fifth?

Established July 3, 1875 in the City of Vicksburg, under title of **Most Worshipful Stringer Grand Lodge, F. & A.M., Prince Hall Affiliation, Jurisdiction of Mississippi.** Location of its Grand East is 1072 John R. Lynch Street, Jackson, Mississippi 39203. Annual communication Sunday before First Tuesday in December. Number of lodges 436, total membership 21,750.

### 27. Twenty-sixth?

Established in Little Rock, March 28, 1873 as "Most Worshipful Grand Lodge F. & A.M." It is now known as **Most Worshipful Prince Hall Grand Lodge F. & A.M. Jurisdiction** of Arkansas. Location of its Grand East is 4th and State Street, Pine Bluff, Arkansas 71601. Annual communication is second Tuesday in August. Number of lodges 185, total membership 7,500.

### 28. Twenty-seventh?

"The Grand Lodge of Connecticut, F. & A.M. (Prince Hall Affiliation)" was instituted on November 3, 1873 in the City of Hartford. Its title is now **Most Worshipful Prince Hall Grand Lodge F. & A.M. of Connecticut, Incorporated.** Location of its Grand East is 106 Goffe Street, New Haven, Connecticut 06511. Annual communication is second Tuesday after First Monday in October. Number of lodges 17, total membership is 1,500.

### 29. Twenty-eighth?

Founded in the year 1851 as the "Widow's Son Grand Lodge of Canada," but is now known as **The Most Worshipful Prince Hall Grand Lodge F. & A.M. Province of Ontario and Jurisdiction.** Location of its Grand East is 7141 Lancaster Avenue, Mississauga, Ontario L4T 2PZ. Annual communication second Monday in August. Number of lodges 11, total membership 1,490.

### 30. Twenty-ninth?

Erected at Brenham, August 19, 1875 as "Grand Lodge F. & A.M." The records also show the date of January 19, 1876 as the date of permanent organization. It is now known as **Most Worshipful Prince Hall Grand Lodge of Texas and Jurisdiction, F. & A.M.** Location of its Grand East is 2851 Evans Street, Fort Worth, Texas 76101. Annual communication is fourth Tuesday in June. Number of lodges 516, total membership 23,320.

### 31. Thirtieth?

"African Grand Lodge of Colorado," founded January 17, 1876 in Denver. Now known as **Most Worshipful Prince Hall**

Grand Lodge F. & A.M. Colorado and Jurisdiction. Location of its Grand East is 1244 Euclid Avenue, Pueblo, Colorado 81004. Annual communication second Monday in August. Number of lodges 13, total membership 929.

### 32. Thirty-first?

"The Most Worshipful Colored Grand Lodge, A.F. & A.M. of West Virginia," was founded in the City of Martinsburg, October 3, 1877. The title was changed to **Prince Hall Grand Lodge F. & A.M. of West Virginia** on March 7, 1919. Location of its Grand East is 513 Elm Street, Institute, West Virginia 25112. Annual communication last Thursday in June. Number of lodges 31, total membership 1,020.

### 33. Thirty-second?

Erected August 9, 1881 at Keokuk as "African Grand Lodge, A.F.& A.M." It later became "United Grand Lodge, A.F. & A.M. of Iowa," when the "African" and "Hiram" grand bodies merged on July 14, 1887 at Des Moines. It is now the **Most Worshipful Prince Hall Grand Lodge F. & A.M. of Iowa and Jurisdiction.** Location of its Grand East is 1340 Idaho Street, Des Moines, Iowa 50306. Annual communication is the second Thursday in July. Number of lodges 15, total membership 646.

### 34. Thirty-third?

"St. John's Grand Lodge A.F. & A.M." was established August 15, 1893 at Ardmore. This Grand Lodge operated until its name was changed in 1947 to **Most Worshipful Prince Hall Grand Lodge F. & A.M. Jurisdiction of Oklahoma.** Location of its Grand East is 5048 North Peoria Street, Tulsa, Oklahoma 74126. Annual communication is the first Sunday in June. Number of lodges 132, total membership 5,000.

### 35. Thirty-fourth?

Established in the City of St. Paul, August 16, 1894 as "Grand Lodge, F. & A.M. of Minnesota." In a special session, June 2, 1950 changed its name to **Most Worshipful Prince Hall Grand Lodge F. & A.M., State of Minnesota and its Jurisdiction.** Location of its Grand East is 3832 4th Avenue South, Minneapolis, Minnesota 55409. Annual communication third Tuesday in September. Number of lodges 10, total membership 701.

### 36. Thirty-fifth?

Organized in Seattle, April 13, 1903 as the "Grand Lodge, F. & A.M. of Washington and Oregon," and later it became "United Grand Lodge." In 1944 it changed its name to the **Most Worshipful Prince Hall Grand Lodge F. & A.M., Washington and Jurisdiction.** Location of its Grand East is 306 24th Avenue, South, Seattle, Washington 98144. Annual communication second Monday in July. Number of lodges 33, total membership 2,200.

### 37. Thirty-sixth?

Erected August 2, 1919 as "Grand Lodge A.F. & A.M. of Nebraska at Lincoln." The Grand Lodge meeting in Omaha July 18-19, 1952 changed its name to **Most Worshipful Prince Hall Grand Lodge F. & A.M. of Nebraska and its Jurisdiction.** Location of its Grand East is 2414 Ames Avenue, Omaha, Nebraska 68111. Annual communication third Wednesday in July. Number of lodges 9, total membership 368.

### 38. Thirty-seventh?

"Sovereign Grand Lodge, F. & A.M." was erected in Phoenix on May 30, 1920. It continued under that name until January 14, 1952, when it amended its charter to become **Most Worshipful Prince Hall Grand Lodge F. & A.M. of the State of Arizona and Jurisdiction, Incorporated.** Location of its Grand East is 2032 Calle Campana De Plata, Tucson, Arizona 85705. Annual communication first Monday in May. Number of lodges 21, total membership 646.

39. Thirty-eighth?

**Prince Hall Grand Lodge F. & A.M. of New Mexico,** after much difficulty with lodges under the authority of sister jurisdictions, was founded in Albuquerque, September 21, 1921. Location of its Grand East is P.O. Box 5358, Albuquerque, New Mexico 87185. Annual communication fourth Monday in June. Number of lodges 13, total membership 263.

40. Thirty-ninth?

Organized in the City of Milwaukee, June 28, 1052 as the **Most Worshipful Prince Hall Grand Lodge, Inc., F. & A.M. of Wisconsin.** Location of its Grand East is 600 West Walnut Street, Suite 30, Milwaukee, Wisconsin 53209. Annual communication third Monday in June. Number of lodges 11, total membership 800.

41. Fortieth?

**Most Worshipful Prince Hall Grand Lodge F. & A.M. of the Commonwealth of the Bahama Islands and Jursidiction, Incorporated.** Erected in 1951. Location of its Grand East is P. O. Box F 3121, Freeport, Grand Bahama, Bahamas. Annual communication nearest Monday to St. John the Baptist Day. Number of lodges 25, total membership 1,345.

42. Forty-first?

**Most Worshipful Prince Hall Grand Lodge, F. & A.M. of Oregon, Incorporated,** organized April 23, 1960, at Portland. Location of its Grand East is 116-20 Northeast Russell Street, Portland, Oregon 97212. Annual communication fourth Monday in June. Number of lodges 8, total membership 269.

43. Forty-second?

**The Most Worshipful Prince Hall Grand Lodge F. & A.M. Jurisdiction of Alaska,** was organized in September 1969 by the Prince Hall Grand Lodge of the State of Washington.

Location of its Grand East is P.O. Box 736, Anchorage, Alaska 99510. Annual communication third Monday in July. Number of lodges 7, total membership 350.

## 44. Forthy-third?

**The Most Worshipful Prince Hall Grand Lodge F. & A.M. of Nevada** was organized in 1980. Location of its Grand East is 2700 Colton Street, North Las Vegas, Nevada 89030. Annual communiction first Sunday in June. Number of lodges 6, total membership 157.

## 45. Forty-fourth?

**M. W. Grand Lodge of Ancient F. & A.M., Republic of Liberia,** organized September 1967. However, no communication has been received from this Grand Lodge since the military coup, which occured April 12, 1980. Prince Hall Freemasonry has been extinguished in this Republic and the leaders of the new military coup killed the Officers of this Grand Lodge.

# Notes for Part Two

1. The following by Harry A. Williamson is of interest, the title being "Exclusive Jurisdiction."

The...title is that of a contribution appearing in the February, 1952, number of *The Masonic World* published at Detroit, Mich., of which James Fairbain Smith is the Editor; the contribution is an address delivered by him upon the subject, as above, before the Masonic Temple Association in January last and of which association he is a Past President.

While that address had particular reference to "Statewide Concurrent Jurisdiction" as affects the lodges in the Michigan jurisdiction, the Past President included reference to "concurrent jurisdiction" as prevails in foreign countries, and, very naturally, these remarks carried an implication pertaining to the "American Doctrine of Exclusive Territorial Jurisdiction," so-called, as prevails within the United States and its direct relationship to the Prince Hall Fraternity.

Several excerpts, as shall now follow, are presented from that address:

1.—"Obviously in those dim distant days there was no such thing known as exlucisve jurisdiction, and as a matter of fact our researches show that here in the city of Detroit, as early as 1770, lodges from the Provincial Grand Lodges of New York, Quebec and two military lodges, warranted by the Grand Lodge of Ireland, were operating in complete harmony in a settlement which then had less than 500 inhabitants."

In commenting upon the foregoing, the Prince Hall Fraternity, along with a number of fairminded white Masonic historians, has contended the warranting of African Lodge No. 459, in 1784, was not and could not have been an "invasion" of the Massachusetts area, because of the customs of the Craft previaling there and in other countries during the 18th century, and the above quotation, tactily confirms that contention.

2—"Even to this day we find in British territories beyond the seas lodges operating side by side under the authority of the Grand Lodges of England, Ireland and Scotland. Thus, to them the doctrine of exclusive jurisdiction is as foreign as it was to the Operative Masons who first asserted their right to the freedoms which the democratic world of today loves so well."

The Prince Hall Fraternity contends that its status as a legitimate Masonic society is not fundamentally affected by that so-called "American Doctrine of Exclusive Territorial Jurisdiction," because of the fact, which is beyond dispute, the white fraternity in the United States is absolutely without any Masonic control over men of color due to the regulation in the codes of at least two Grand Lodges; the decisions of several of the Grand Masters of various Grand Lodges together with the general practice of the other grand bodies, all of which deny or forbid the initiation of men whose skin has been kissed by the rays of Africa's sun.

American Masonry has proclaimed to the entire Masonic world that its teachings are for the exclusive use of white men. The Past President amply illustrates the fact that outside of the United States and Canada there is no bar to concurrent Jurisdictions as relates to the four largest Masonic Constitutions, namely: England, Ireland, Scotland and the Netherlands either at home or overseas.

Observe what the Past President says further:

3.—"No one can quarrel with the doctrine of exclusive jurisdiction as it affects the borders of a state, but when it is used to define the actual jurisdiction of a single lodge, then it would appear that the old traditions of the early Freemasons are being thrown completely into the discard. Even today in Britain men may elect to join wherever they desire, and thus we find English men joining Scottish lodges, and conversely, Scots joining English lodges, and it is done without the slightest degree of discontention."

For an instant let us examine into the situation in at least four foreign countries, namely Egypt, where both England and Scotland have lodges, also, in West Africa. In India, England, Ireland and Scotland have lodges in the East Indies and similarly, in South Africa, with Netherlands, they have lodges which, in many instances, have members from lodges under the several Constitutions and nobody's feelings is injured.

Among the American grand bodies, territorial jurisdiction rests, in a few instances, with the desires of a particular Grand Lodge; for example: New York has lodges in the Near East; Massachusetts has lodges in both Panama and Chile.

4—"Once again, let me stress the fact that if Masonry in the 18th century had been curbed by the petty concept of exclusive jurisdiction, it could never have spread to the four corners of the world. Actually, Masonry at the time, considered the whole world its jurisdiction."

(Williamson's Italics)

In view of the first sentence in the above quotation, it is well to state that if the American Negro had paid any attention to the jurisdictional curbs on racial lines as have been invented by the white American Craft, he would, even at this late date, still be deprived of the teachings and benefits of Ancient Craft Masonry.

The question is now asked: supposing the Negro had been the dominant racial group in the United States and his lodge had refused to initiate white men, what would the latter have done? Who will answer this?

Another excerpt reads:

5—"Jealousies which were rampant among the colonists who asserted their independence of the Mother Country in 1776 brought into being the desire for Independent Grand Lodges and it was this new found authority on the part of American Masons which brought into being the doctrine of Exclusive Jurisdiction.

"In other words, it was their desire, by means, to stop forever the erection of English, Scottish and Irish lodges within the borders of the 13 original states. Nay, more the new independent Grand Lodges even legislated against each other, and as a result, the new jurisdictional trend was even given impetus by the subordinate Lodge."

Suppose, even at this late date, the Grand Lodges in England, Ireland or Scotland should erect a lodge or lodges within the boundaries of any one or more of the American States, what could the Grand Lodge already established therein do about it? The only thing the Grand Lodge could do would be to sever fraternal relations with the offending foreign Grand Lodge and what great loss would the latter suffer thereby?

The remainder of the contribution from which the foregoing excerpts have been taken deals primarily to the subject of *Lodge* concurrent jurisdiction as it affects the White Craft in Michigan, and consequently, is without any bearing upon the character of the discussion which shall now follow.

During the course of an extensive research into the subject covering a period of many years, it is evident there are very few Masonic historians, past and present, who had or who have any accurate knowledge of the origin of the so called territorial jurisdiction, also, that such was unknown in the United States until the very last portion of the 18th century. One need only to examine any edition of a well-known international directory of Masonic lodges to learn how concurrent jurisdiction works outside of the North American Continent without the slightest degree of irritation among foreign Grand Lodges.

Even during a portion of the 19th century, this doctrine, so-called, was not rigidly adhered to by some Grand Lodges.

In all probability, the very first record of what can be construed as constituting exclusive territorial jurisdiction was an agreement entered into between the Grand Masters of England and Holland about 1770, whereby each agreed not to erect a lodge within the geographical confines of the other.

Without doubt the earliest record of a similar agreement or attempt to prevent invasion of another territory, can be found in the

*Proceedings* of the Grand Lodge of New York for 1794, for, under the date of December 7th, in that year, the following can be found:

"The Right Worshipful the Deputy Grand Master reported the reply recommended by the Committee (appointed at the last meeting) to be made to the Grand Lodge of the State of Massachusetts, which was unanimously approved.

"In consequence of the report from the above Committee being adopted, the following resolve was entered into:

"*Whereas*, the Grand Lodge of the State of Massachusetts have, by a communication dated the 4th of January, 1796, suggested to this Grand Lodge the adopting a regulation declaring that no charter or dispensation for holding a Lodge be issued by any Grand Lodge to any number of Masons residing out of the State wherein the Grand Lodge is established."

"Be it therefore

*Resolved* and declared by this Grand Lodge, That no charter or dispensation for holding a lodge of Masons, be ever granted to any person or persons, whatsoever, residing out of this State and within the jurisdiction of any other Grand Lodge."

The above language indicates that Massachusetts must have submitted a suggestion at an earlier date, because, a similar item along this line can be found in the *Proceedings* of the Grand Lodge of Massachusetts under the date of September 10, 1794, and it reads:

"Voted, That the Grand Secretary be instructed to write to the Grand Lodge in the State of Rhode Island informing them that it is the intention and full determination of this Grand Lodge, not to grant any charter of erection to any Lodge out of this commonwealth, where another Grand Lodge has jurisdiction, hinting to them the absolute necessity of the measure, and requesting them to join in a plan so likely to operate to the benefit of Masonry in general."

After a search of the records of the Grand Lodge of Rhode Island, an official thereof has written as follows:

"I can find no record of the Grand Lodge of Rhode Island taking any action in regard to territorial jurisdiction between States in the early days.

"If the Grand Secretary of Massachusetts did address our Grand Lodge after the date of September 19, 1794, there apparently was no record made of his address.

"The early records are very scanty."

There is no stretching of the truth in saying that when the subject of the Freemasonry of the Negro in this country became an active and nationwide topic, those in the White Fraternity who were steeped in both race and color prejudice, dug up this doctrine, so-called, and deliberately, with malice aforethought, diverted the same from its original intention as an excellent vehicle for the sole purpose of discrediting the Prince Hall Fraternity. This statement cannot be denied by anyone truthfully.

Over the years many of the leaders of the White Fraternity in this country have claimed that the "American Doctrine of Exclusive Territorial Jurisdiction" is a fundamental regulation within their branch of the institution, but not a single historian has ever produced indisputable records to prove that the Grand Lodges ever held a joint convention, or, that any group of them has ever offically adopted such to become the fundamental law of any number of grand bodies. Such, never having been done, how can it be classified as representing fundamental Masonic law?

Two records extant clearly indicate that some of the Grand Lodges did not recognize such a law. These were as follows:

(a) This has been transcribed from the *Virginia Text Book* compiled by John Dove, edition of 1920, Section 1, page 31:

"The limitation of her [Va.] jurisdiction, set out in subsequent sections, are conceded in a spirit of comity and fraternity to her sister Grand Lodges, *but with a resolution of right at any time hereafter to recall the concession.*

*(Williamson's Italics)*

(b) The second illustration can be found in the *Proceedings* of Grand Lodge of Tennessee, Volume 1, page 223, of the records between 1813 and 1847. In 1829, the Grand Master of the Grand Lodge of Louisiana addressed a communication to the Grand Master of the Grand Lodge of Kentucky, which reads, in part, as follows:

"According to the rules, principles and usages of Masonry which now govern the Craft in the United States and define the different jurisdictions, is or is not the Grand Lodge of each State supreme within such State?

Is it competent for the Grand Lodge of those States to institute Lodges within another State in which a regular Grand Lodge already exists?"

The Grand Master of the Grand Lodge of Kentucky referred the matter to a committee and it submitted the following statement:

"Beg leave to report that in their opinion, agreeably to the principles and usages of Masonry, the jurisdiction of a Grand Lodge, duly constituted, *is not confined to territorial limits, but it is competent for a Grand Lodge in one State to excerise jurisdiction in another, although there may be a Grand Lodge already established there.* This is however, merely a question of power, and not of policy or comity, or the manner in jurisdiction should be exercised, *respecting which no opinion is expressed.*"

*(Williamson's Italics)*

Upon the allegedly important "doctrine" the foregoing records reveal there has never been any concerted action by the American Grand Lodges.

Because of the general attitude toward the Prince Hall Fraternity upon the promise of this alleged principle of exclusive jurisdiction and because of the refusal of the White Fraternity in America to grant Masonic status to that organization, the Whites amply illustrate the fact their conception of Masonry is nothing more or less than a hollow mockery and reminds one of the 12th Chapter of the First Epistle of Paul, the Apostle to the Corinthians.

Such of the American rituals which have come to attention reveal that American Masonry teaches at least two important facts to its candidates, to wit:

(a) That Masonry regards no man on account of his *RACE,* creed or *COLOR.*

(b) Masonry unites men of every country, *SECT* and opinion.

Because of its color bar, the question is asked in all sincerity, how can American Masonry make "precept" coincide with "practice?" Further, since the Holy Bible is such an indispensable part of the furniture of a lodge and the candidate is directed to govern his life in accordance with its teachings, it might not be a bad idea for American Masonry to remove the Bible from the Altars of its lodges, because the members thereof make no attempt to live in accordance with the *contents* therein.

2. In the *Masonic Square,* published by A. Lewis in England, March and June 1982 issues, volume 8 on page 39 of the first issue records that the Grand Lodge of Massachusetts had issued a small folder for

everyone, to present current information...It further states that "The Grand Lodge of Masons in Massachusetts is the oldest Grand Lodge in the Western hemisphere, dating back to 1733 when Henry Price was appointed Provincial Grand Master for New England by warrant from Lord Montague in England."

In reply to that letter was printed on page 81 of the later issue: The statement...that "the Grand Lodge of Massachusetts is the oldest Grand Lodge in the Western hemisphere" cannot be allowed to stand. The correct position is shown on page 18 of *A Register of Grand Lodges Active and Extinct* published by the Masonic Service Association. "...The control of Freemasonry was first established in Massachusetts on 30 July 1733 with the appointment of Henry Price as Provincial Grand Master, but that appointment did not create a Grand Lodge in any shape or form. This Provincial Grand Lodge remained under England until April 1787 when it declared itself to be a Grand Lodge. Alongside of this was the Provincial Grand Lodge under Scotland, formed on 27 December 1769 and it, in turn, declared itself on 8 March 1777 to be a Grand Lodge. Both Grand Lodges amalgamated on 19 March 1782 to form the present Grand Lodge of Massachusetts. At the most, it can claim existence from 1787—certainly not from 1773."

3. To show the confusion of the minutes of African Lodge, Harry A. Williamson notes that "the first reference in this micro-film to a *Grand Lodge* appears on August 17, 1826, when the subject of the Lodge at Providence, R.I. was discussed." However, this writer has the photocopy of the minutes of African Lodge, which shows that African Lodge No. 459 met August 21, 1826 which reads: "...after which there was a committee chosen to go from this lodge to Providence to examine the lodge there." There is little doubt that we are dealing with a number of minutes of African Lodge, which have been transcribed incorrectly.

4. Here again, the records are not at all clear. Prince Hall in his letter book, wrote a letter to "Mr. Peter Mantore" stating that "we are willing to set you at work under our charter and Lodge No. 459, from London; under that authority, and by the name of the African Lodge, we hereby and herein give you license to assemble and work as aforesaid, under that denomination as in the sight and fear of God." The record is not clear or concise. Some of the minutes of the Prince Hall Masons in Pennsylvania ended up in the record books of African Lodge in Boston. How this came about has ever remained a mystery.

This writer will not debate the regularity of this, pointing to Mother Kilwinning, Lodge Melrose St. John and the revolution and assumption of the Grand Lodge of Massachusetts.

Pennsylvania probably is the oldest Grand Lodge within the Prince Hall Masonic family, established in Philadelphia on December 27, 1815, "First Independence African Grand Lodge F. & A.M. of Pennsylvania." African Lodge No. 459 established by the Boston African Lodge was the first Lodge, Union No. 2, founded June 8, 1810, was the second. Laurel No. 5, 1881, the third. And the fourth was Phoenix No. 6, 1814.

The "First Independent African Grand Lodge" was succeeded by the "United Grand Lodge, A.F. & A.M." at a convention held December 26, 1882 in Philadelphia, when the rival Grand Lodges consolidated into the present Grand Lodge. There is considerable difficulty in researching the records of this body. It does, however, seem that in 1837, Union No. 2 and Harmony No. 5 and others organized the "Hiram Grand Lodge of Pennsylvania" and under that title they participated in the formation of the "National Grand Lodge of North America," at a convention at Boston, Masscahusetts in 1847.

It appears that some time prior to 1837, the two Lodges mentioned had either withdrawn or had been expelled from the "First Independent African Grand Lodge." In 1848, the "Hiram Grand Lodge" and the "First Independent African Grand Lodge" merged and became the **Grand Lodge for the State of Pennsylvania.** The "Hiram Grand Lodge" was referred generally as the "Seventh Street Masons" because it met in a hall on that street, and the "First Independent African Grand Lodge" was known as the "Eleventh Streeters" for the same reason.

In 1849, dissatisfaction set in due in part by the "auto-cratic" practices of the officials of the National Grand Lodge, and former members of the Hiram group withdrew from the new body until unification in 1882. This was the beginning of the decline and final dissolution of the National Compact some 30 years later.

In other Masonic proceedings, this body was known as the "Hiram Organization of Pennsylvania." There is much concerning this Grand Lodge which is yet unknown, and it had not published its history. Until such time as a definitive study of Afro-American history, there will continue to be many blank spots and much that is not known. There has been a considerable amount of material written on this subject by those who are far removed from knowledge of the proper study of Afro-American history, and to those who would pass judgment concerning the Masonic history of Prince Hall Freemasonry in Pennsylvania, that subject remains controversial.

My comments that Pennsylvania probably was the oldest Grand Lodge within the Prince Hall Masonic family stirred up a hornet's nest and ended up being debated on the floor of the Conference of Prince Hall Grand Masters. I was roundly taken to task for my statement and there was much misunderstanding as to why I made the claim. So perhaps I should attempt to explain the why of it all.

Some years ago, I purchased from Mr. John M. Sherman of the Caucasian Grand Lodge of Massachusetts a microfilm copy of the minutes of African Lodge No. 459. However, not trusting Mr. Sherman, I thought it wise that I receive an actual photocopy of the minutes of African Lodge. While the Prince Hall Grand Lodge of Massachusetts was not aware of this, I had the actual minutes of African Lodge placed on a photocopier and reproduced. The minutes of African Lodge No. 459 begins December 28, 1807 and tracks through many meetings—the most interesting being held January 13, 1823 and reads: "The African Lodge No. 459 met it being a regular meeting at which time Bro. John T. Hilton was Crafted and a number of visiting Brothers of the City was present." This was John Telemachus Hilton, a man of exceptional ability.

The minutes of February 10, 1823 reads "The African Lodge No. 459 greeting. This evening the Lodge met and Brother John T. Hilton was raised to the Sublime degree of a master mason and paid for the same which was deposited in the box." In 1826 Bro. Hilton would be elected Master of the Lodge.

On the 21st of January 1826 the Lodge received a letter from Boyer Lodge in New York City requesting a Charter for a Lodge and a committee was appointed to investigate the matter. On 21 August "After which time was a committee chosen to go from this Lodge to Providence to examine the Lodge there then if found worthy to give them a Charter or warrant..." On September 11th, 1826, "there was a vote past (sic) that the committee should not go on to Providence until they had more information from there." On September 18th "there was a committee chosen to write a letter to Providence in answer to one received from our Masonic Brethren in respecting a committee going on to visit them which is to be determined at our next meeting.

At the 25 September 1826 meeting "the letter written by the committee chosen in answer to the one from our Brethren at Providence was read to the satisfaction of the Brethren present." October 9th, 1826 "the lodge was visited by Brother George G. Willis & Brother Pero

Martin from Providence." The two Brothers had brought a letter which was read and discussed. On October 23, 1826, a committee was then chosen consisting of the W. Master J. T. Hilton and two others to "settle with the committee which was sent on to New York to establish there a Lodge which committee consisted of then W.M. L. H. Moody (and others). Their decisions were to be satisfactory to the Lodge and a final conclusion."

At the October 30th, 1826 meeting, "The money was received from the commity (sic Committee) that was chosen to go [to] Providence and paid into the Lodge, sixteen dollars. The commity (sic) did not go. A petition was received from our brethren in Providence praying for a warrant to empowering them to work as a Lodge. The petition was read, and a commity (sic) chosen to act upon the same. Voted that the brethren in Providence shall have their warrant without paying except their yearly tribute. That the commity (sic) shall have three dollars a day while and there (?) that they shall send a letter to the Brethren at Providence to inform of said vote and request them to write when they shall be ready."

The minutes of June 18th, 1827 read: "First a proposition was made to the lodge by the committee who went to N. York desiring to know what would satisfy this Lodge. Should they give an independent Charter to the Boyer Lodge and the Lodge unanimously agreed to be satisfied with two hundred dollars on the delivery of the Charter alluded to, the Boyer Lodge No. 1, City of N. York to the Grand African Lodge No. 459. The proposition having been accepted by the Lodge, the Lodge proceeded to and did declare themselves Independent of any Lodge in the known world and then agreed to grant to the Boyer Lodge No. 1 N. York the Independent Charter according to agreement. The W. Master and J. T. Hilton was chosen to write and publish the declaration of Independence. He was given the privilege to make a choice of whom he thought proper to assist him and also to write the Independent Charter. Brothers J. T. Hilton and Thomas Paul was chosen by the Lodge to proceed to N. York with the Charter and have their passage paid for their time. To Brother Hilton a dollar a day for 6 days, to Bro. Paul 2 dollars a day for 6 days."

The famous declaration of Independence appeared in the *Boston Daily Advertiser* on the 26th of June, signed by the Master, the Senior and Junior Wardens and the Secretary.

From June the 25th, 1827 the minutes note that the Lodge is now called The African Grand Lodge No. 459. The minutes of 10 July 1827 reads: "The Grand African Lodge met in case of emergecy opened on the first degree. When the Committee of New York, report that the Boyer Lodge No. 1 refused to accept the charter and without much satisfaction to the Comittee, it was then voted that the M.W. Master E. A. De Randamie, to write to Boyer Lodge No. 1 for further explanation of their conduct." The minutes of 26 August 1827 had the Master read the letter that he had drafted and it was approved by the Lodge. 'It was also noted that "the M.W. Master De Randamie, Brother Past Master S.G. Moody and Brother Pastmaster Hilton be a committee to prepare an Independent Charter for the Grand African Lodge agreeable to their Declaration in the newspaper."

This goes to show that African Lodge No. 459 became a "Mother" Grand Lodge in 1827, and in so doing, it did what other lodges had done before her.

# PART THREE

# The "National Grand Lodge"

**1. The National Grand Lodge or "Compact" was formed in 1847. What can be said of it?**

The National Grand Lodge or "Compact," unlike the several attempts to organize a General Grand Lodge in the United States by mainstream Freemasonry[1] or Rob Morris's "strange" Conservators,[2] was a "peculiarity" of Prince Hall Freemasonry. It was organized for survival during a period in American history that was particularly harsh for Black America. For instance, in 1847, the year of its birth, in Philadelphia was one of the Grand Lodges that was deeply involved in the organization of the "Compact." There were only 20,000 Blacks living in Philadelphia, of which 11,000 were in central Philadelphia. Of this number approximately 4,000 were domestic servants; the rest mostly laborers, artisans, coachmen, expressmen and barbers. Out of the 4,446 Black children 1,888 were enrolled in schools in the city, 504 were at work or apprentices and 2,074 were at home or unaccounted for—one example of the harshness of the times. Another example: a White gang, known as the "Killers of Moyamensing" led an armed raid on Blacks in Philadelphia. The militia had to be called out to contain them.

A year earlier, a petition by a group of Whites and Blacks to the Boston School Committee for the opening of public schools to Blacks was refused. A Black sued the city of Boston on behalf of his 5 year old daughter, asking for damages because the city refused to allow her in a White public school, to no avail.

The case went to the Supreme Court of Massachusetts which rejected the appeal and established in its direction the precedent for the controversial "separate and equal" doctrine in the U.S. law. The 1793 Federal Fugitive Law, which provided for the extradition of criminals, allowed a "master" to seize his runaway slave in another State, take him before a magistrate and acquire authority to take him home was still on the booPs and Blacks, many of them "free" were being kidnapped off the streets. In 1850 this law was strengthened to allow any claimants to take possession of a Black upon establishing proof of ownership before a federal commissioner. No safeguards such as jury trial or judicial hearing for the captive, were included. The Act provided fines of $1,000 and imprisonment for six months of citizens or officials who failed to aid in the capture of fugitives.

Within 36 hours of passage of the Fugitive Slave Law, 40 Massachusetts Blacks departed for Canada, and the Black population of other states dropped. Missouri, like many other slave states, forbade the instruction of Blacks in reading or writing and, in Virginia, the law stated that the right of citizenship in the State was confined to free White persons only.

Even during hostile times, individual Prince Hall Freemasons, like the Grand Lodges themselves, excelled. In St. Louis, Missouri, Rev. Moses Dickson, who would later serve as Grand Master of the Prince Hall Grand Lodge of Missouri, with 11 other Blacks, formed a secret and militant organization: The Knights of Liberty. They agreed to disperse for ten years to form secret socities to emancipate the Blacks. They would grow to 47,240, and since Prince Hall Freemasonry was the only organized interstate organization outside the church, in all likelihood the organization was formed within the lodges. Bro. Robert Morris of Boston and Bro. George B. Vashon, both Prince Hall Freemasons, graduates of Oberlin College, were admitted to the Bar. Vashon also taught classics at New York Central College. Past Master Martin R. Delany was admitted to Harvard Medical School and John V. DeGrasse, later a Grand Master of Massachusetts, began the study of medicine at Bowdoin College.

It is only against the background of the "madness" of that year that the formation of the National Grand Lodge or "Compact," can be placed into proper perspective. Those critics who attempt to view the Freemasonry of the Black man in American in the same vein as mainstream American Freemasonry cannot comprehend that they are dealing with two Americas and two peoples, who had little in common. Though the laws of Freemasonry as derived from England may have had strict guidelines, they could hardly apply to a people who lived in the racist atmosphere that existed during that period. Prince Hall Masons looked for survival more than precedents in Masonic regulations.[3]

What follows is excerpted from my unpublished Manuscript of the history of the Prince Hall Grand Lodge of Louisiana.[4]

## NATIONALISM

The National Grand Lodge was a phenomenon of Prince Hall Freemasonry. Defining it within strict confines of Masonry is impossible, but with the circumscription of the Black experience it is somewhat understandable. It is as much an American peculiarity, oddity, and curiosity as the doctrine of "Exclusive Territorial Jurisdiction" or Rob Morris's Conservators Movement which swept mainstream American Masonry.[5] Neither can be defined within the strict confines of Masonic law or fully justified; both are debatably un-Masonic and yet they happened.

During the Masonic career of George Washington, the mainstream Grand Lodges considered the formation of a single National or General Grand Lodge with Washington proposed as the National Grand Master. This idea never materialized.[6] On the other hand, what transpired in Prince Hall Freemasonry to this day remains subject of debate and controversy.

In 1847, there were lodges in Boston, New York, Philadelphia, Delaware and other areas, but there was a "general lack of knowledge of the principles which should govern Masons, individually or collectively."[7] For instance, the lodges in New York City held no fraternal intercourse with each other and there was a general lack of fraternal feeling and cooperation among these Prince Hall bodies.

The problem was deplorable, and it was felt that something had to be done. With the celebration of the feast of St. John approaching, it was thought that it would be an ideal time to establish stronger fraternal ties between the several lodges. John T. Hilton of Boston, and a few others, decided to call together as many of the Prince Hall Masons from the various lodges as possible. The purpose was for exchanging ideas and to participate in a grand celebration to be held after the first meeting of the convention.

What actually transpired remains a controversy. Bro. Alexander Elston of the United Grand Lodge of New York, who was present and took part at the convention stated that:

> "Though the convention desired and sought to bring about a more fraternal feeling between the different Lodges...a National Grand Lodge, or formal compact, was not mentioned or introduced at any time in that convention."

Bro. Elston further explained that:

> "The convention was called to order by J. T. Hilton as chairman, who stated that the object of the call was to form a *union* and to celebrate the anniversary of St. John the Baptist [Day] by a street parade and an oration. The oration was delivered by the chairman, J. T. Hilton. The convention met on the 23rd of June, adjourned to the 25th, in order that all might take part in the celebration on the 24th, came together again on the 25th and adjourned without anything being said or done about a national compact, or National Grand Lodge..."

In 1849, the Committee on Correspondence of the United Grand Lodge of New York of which Bro. Elston was a member, issued the following statement:

> "In the first place we shall have to go back as far as the year 1847. The lodges at that time existing among us in the City of New York, were separate and distant bodies,

holding no intercourse with each other, and cherishing in many instances hatred, where love should exist between them, when they were cheered with the intelligence that a call had been issued by John T. Hilton, M.W. Grand Master of a body styling itself the 'African Grand Lodge of Massachusetts'[9] inviting the fraternity of colored Masons to assemble on a certain day, specified in the call (to unite as the heart of one man), in the City of Boston, State of Massachusetts, for the purpose of forming a permanent relation or union; which convention was holden at the time and place designated, and resolutions were passed, and everything that was deemed necessary in the preliminary state of the affair was agreed upon, and the convention adjourned *sine die.*

Now mark what follows!

A delegation from Philadelphia which was not in time to participate in the *regular business* [in] which they were expected to aid by their counsel and their well-known devotion to the cause, finding that the convention had suspended it labors, by and with the consent of the original callers of the convention, did attempt to re-organize the convention, a body to all intents and purposes dead in law and in fact; and they did then and there, in the face of all right, and in open violation of the good faith which ought to and did exist at the time and did to all intents and purpose, contrary to the intentions and meaning of the original call.

And the result of the deliberation of the second convention was the formation of that *anomaly*, or rather "NONDESCRIPT" in Masonry, a National Grand Lodge for these United States, to have jurisdiction over and hold in *subordination* the Grand Lodges of the several States: thus setting themselves up as KINGS and PRINCES in Masonry, but virtually making objects of *ridicule* to every intelligent, upright, consistent and well-informed Mason. And further to give the gloss of legality to their acts, they set forth that at a solemn convention of three State Grand

Lodges, convened for the purpose, in the City of Boston, and State of Massachusetts, on a certain day of June, 1847, they entered into a bond of union and formed a National Grand Lodge. At the same time they must have been aware that their action was *illegal, unconstitutional* and a removal of the *ancient landmarks* of the Order.[10]

Whether from the first meeting of the convention or from a second "unauthorized" meeting the following document was issued:

### Declaration of Sentiment
### of the
### Great National Convention

Held in the City of Boston, State of Massachusetts, on the 24th, 25th, 26th and 28th days of June, A.L. 5847 — A.D. 1847.

Sentiment 1: The question has been asked: the cause of the separate organizations of white and colored Masons in the United States of America? We do not know of any good reason why there should be, and we have made several attempts, without any success, to have but one. We are, and always have been, in possession of all the ancient landmarks and regulations of the Craft; and we do acknowledge all genuine Masons, of all nations and shades of complexion, to be our brethren.

Sentiment 2: Therefore, in pursuance of the above call, we have met in the City of Boston, State of Massachusetts, in the year and date above mentioned, and do form in convention, and lay before the world our sentiments thereon.

Sentiment 3: In all stages of oppression, we have petitioned for redress, but found none, *therefore*, in solemn convention assembled, we do, in the name of the Great Masonic Body of Free and Accepted A.Y. Masons declare ourselves a free and independent body of Masons, to be known as the National Grand Lodge of Free and Accepted Ancient York Masons (Colored) of the United States of America, and Masonic jurisdiction, thereunto belonging, with full power and authority to grant warrants of constitution to all State Grand Lodges under our jurisdiction, and that the said State Grand Lodges shall have full power and authority to grant letters of dispensation and warrants of constitution to subordinate Lodges within their several jurisdictions, and to establish as many Lodges as they may deem most expedient.

Sentiment 4: Not that we have been wanting in attention to our white brethren, we have from time to time solicited them to extend their jurisdiction over us, but to no effect.

We, therefore, the delegates of the several Lodges throughout these United States, in convention assembled, appealing to the Supreme Judge of the World for the rectitude of our intentions, do, in the name, and by the authority of our constituents, declare and publish the said National Grand Lodge, (Colored) of the United States to be a *Free and Independent body*, with full powers, as named in the third article of this declaration; and for the support of this declaration, with a firm reliance on the protection of Divine Providence, we mutually pledge ourselves to each other in the solemn ties of Brotherhood.

Your Committee most respectfully recommends to your honorable body, the *Free Mason's Library and General Ahiman's Rezon*, as published in 1826, for your government for the next ensuing six months, or the time being, and that the eighth article or the eighth section shall in no cause or instance be departed from.[11]

Delegates:

    Boston, Mass.,—John T. Hilton, George Gall,
       Wm. E. Ambush, Nathan Lewis, George C.
       Willis, Henry Harris, James H. Holt
       Thomas Dalton.

    New York.—Alexander Elston, Wm. H. Clark,
       L. Hayden.

    Providence, R.I.,—Nathan C. Willis

    Pennsylvania—Samuel Van Brakle, Emery

Cronacon, James Newsman, Phillip
Buchanan, Jonathan Lopeman, J. W.
Powell, Wm. H. Bruce, John Anderson,
James J. G. Bias, M.D., James Bird,
James J. Richmond.

Committee[12]

Aldrage B. Cooper, P.G.M., Grand Historian of the
Prince Hall Grand Lodge of New Jersey, noted that:

> "*With an incomprehensible* flair for employing a
> misnomer and for approving an historical untruth, that
> body, allegedly formed, was formally titled viz: "The Na-
> tional Grand Lodge of Free and Accepted Ancient York
> Masons of the United States of North America and the
> Masonic Jurisdiction Thereunto Belonging."

There must be a pause for momentary examination of a
part of that imposing title. There are no records extant,
nor do any recognized authorities of this day or any other
day indicate in the least that there ever have been any
records which purport to show that any Negroes in this
country ever were given the degrees of Masonry under the
auspices of the so-called 'Antient' Grand Lodge of
England. Neither was any Lodge of Negroes ever instituted under the aegis of the Grand Lodge of England
that was commonly termed, although incorrectly so, 'An-
tients'. Nor was any group of Negroes chartered in this
country under the protection of the legitimate 'Antient
York Masons' in this country by Thomas Smith Webb.[13]

Willis N. Brent, a Grand Master (1879-1882) of Missouri,
Grand Secretary in 1883, and a writer of note, in his annual
address as Grand Master in 1880, noted:

> "Is it necessary to disprove the pretentions of our
> misguided brethren? A smile of derision mounts the cheek
> of every Mason who is conversant with the history of Free
> Masonry among Colored men. It is a confession of fraud
> and irregularity to advertize ourselves as Ancient York
> Masons...The title Ancient York was a fiction invented by

J. T. Hilton and his co-adjutors and, like their assumption of national supremacy, was intended to overawe and mislead."[14]

The Constitution of the National Grand Lodge was written in such a manner as to destory absolutely the complete sovereignty of individual Grand Lodges.

"Article 1: ...hereby declared to be the highest legitimate source of Masonic authority (colored) of and over the three symbolic degrees of Free Masonry within its jurisdiction; and...exercises jurisdiction and government over all symbolic Grand Lodges (colored) within the United States of North America. And no such M.W. Grand Lodge can exist or exercise any Masonic privileges or duty, within the United States without the sanction of this M.W.N. Grand Lodge, by warrant duly granted for that purpose. And all convocations or assemblies of persons calling themselves Lodges of Free Masons, in any of said States, of either or all of the three symbolic degrees, without the sanction of this M.W.N. Grand Lodge first had or obtained, are hereby declared to be spurious or clandestine, and of no Masonic authority whatever."[15]

Cooper noted that "It must be recognized that for any Grand Lodge to delegate its authority or to recognize any other authority save its own in the discharge of Masonic function and remain a sovereign Grand Lodge is impossible."

"That is fundamental. At best there could have existed a loosely-bound federation whose acts would have been merely of an advisory nature, and whose findings and agreements would have no force or effect upon the individual Grand Lodges unless these were arrived at separately and sanctioned by the individual Grand Lodges themselves. Any admission to the contrary would disturb the entire constitutional foundation upon which Grand Lodges of Freemasons are established. For Grand Lodges of Freemasons may recognized no other Masonic authoirty save their own. The dissenter from the plan of the

National Grand Lodge apparently understood that principle. The National Compact from the very beginnings exceeded its authority and strayed beyond its Masonic bounds."[16]

For whatever purpose the National Grand Lodge was formed it created nothing but dissension among Prince Hall Freemasonry. On the floor of the National Grand Lodge meeting in Baltimore in 1865, the following report was read:

"That there exists an unhappy disunion in the Masonic fraternity is a source of deep regret. The cause of this division, we think, is no doubt attributable to the irregularities that have crept into the fraternity, for the want of proper instructions relating to the laws and principles of the institution, especially in the organization of the 'National Grand Lodge,' which destroyed, we think, one of the great principles of the fraternity in the government of the Craft, by claiming the right to hold Grand Lodges and Grand Masters subordinate to its decrees.

"We are fully satisifed that the time has arrived when there should be a unity of feeling and sentiment on this question among Masons, because we are placed in a very different position from any other class of men in the country, and for the additional reasons that no matter what may be our difference today, we all emanated from the same original source, and are laboring to attain the same common end—the elevation of our fellow man.

"Your committee are of the opinion, that an honorable *union*, without compromising any cardinal principle of the ancient usages and customs of the fraternity, ought to be formed. They think, that should the system of government known as the 'National Grand Lodge,' be abandoned by the body, the Grand Lodges in the several states could immediately take measures to unite upon the basis of common Masonic usage, for the government of the Craft."[17]

Such resolutions coming before the National Grand Lodge were rejected out-and-out.

Although the National Grand Lodge had solemnly covenated to respect the territory and jurisdiction of the existing grand bodies, it violated this agreement in 1848 by permitting its officers to establish a second Grand Lodge in New York and other states.[18]

In an *Address to the Colored Masonic Fraternity* by William T. Boyd, he detailed that:

In 1855 it established a Grand Lodge in the State of Delaware in violation of the rights of the original Grand Lodge of that State which had been in existence nearly six years.

It has established a second Grand Lodge in Maryland in that State.

It has taken upon itself prerogative of State Grand Lodges in issuing warrants to Subordinate Lodges, *viz.*, one in Portsmouth and two others in Rhode Island, which are claimed in its minutes as being under its exclusive jurisdiction.

In 1866 the National Grand Master, on application of sundry individuals, organized a Grand Lodge at Norfolk, Va., instead of leaving it to be a voluntary act of a convention of the Lodges of that State...

In June, 1863, the Lodges of Louisiana in a legal manner, organized a Grand Lodge which objected to the extensive power exercised by the National Grand Lodge and, in 1865, sent a memorial to the National Grand Lodge setting forth its views and complaining of the exercise of these powers without any adequate good results as a compensation. This memorial was slighted—no effect was made to justify or to palliate them in any manner to give satisfaction and, in 1867, R.H. Gleaves issued his autocratic manifesto forbidding all Masons in any manner to fellowship with or recognize Louisiana Masons;...He established a Subordinate Lodge in Louisiana where there was a Grand Lodge already established.[19]

During the years 1875 three important conventions of Prince Hall Freemasons were held. On June 23rd, 1875 members of the fraternity gathered in Boston, Massachusetts to lay plans for the Centennial Celebration of the initiation of Prince Hall. The convention recommended "that a more perfect union be formed by our Craft and, believing that the spirit of the age in which we live and our duty to the people demand a cordial relationship to each other, to entitle it to the respect of the whole country." [20]

A second convention was held in Chicago, Illinois, September 4-6, 1877. Fifteen Grand Lodges were represented.[21] The attendance was larger than the convention held in Boston the previous year. The purpose of the convention was to "investigate the cause of the separate systems of Grand Lodges and to attempt to bring about a more perfect union," and:

"1. On account of the discord, to some extent prevalent among colored Masons and the American Continent;... having the prosperity of the Craft at heart, deem it expedient, for the purpose of effecting a complete Union, and to harmonize, if possible, the entire Craft, it issued this call for a National Masonic Convention.

2. To investigate the cause of the separate [systems of] Grand Lodges of Colored Masons in the United States of America, and devise suitable measures for the removal of all present differences.

3. In order that we may bring about a more perfect union, that is so much desired among us, we must remove the cause of division. We must endeavor, with our utmost exertions, to cement the craft in every State; and we respectfully invite the co-operation of all officers and members of the Grand Lodges and Subordinate Lodges in the country."[22]

After much debate several resolutions were agreed upon.

"Resolved, That it is the sense of Convention that every Grand Lodge is sovereign."

The second resolution which made a declaration confirming the geographical limits of each Grand Lodge:

"Resolved, Where two Grand Lodges now exist in any State or territory holding concurrent jurisdiction therein, they shall meet in convention of all subordinate Lodges constituting such Grand Lodges to form one Grand Lodge..."

This resolution identical in principle with the Caucasian American doctrine of "exclusive jurisdiction" received general condemnation: "The resolution is identical in principle with the American doctrine of 'exclusive jurisdiction.' It announces that, Each Grand Lodge [American White Grand Lodges] has sole and exclusive Masonic jurisdiction throughout the limits of the State or Territory within which it is regularly established. There can be but *one* legal Grand Lodge in any State or Territory.

"If we accept this doctrine, which is repudiated by all Masonic powers throughout the world, save those upon the American Continent, what becomes of our own Masonic existence? It may seem to bridge over present difficulties, but it leads us to a precipice from which we can neither advance nor retreat. Geographical boundaries do not constitute a Grand Lodge; it is a moral essence, and exists so long as the membership which adheres to it exists and claims."

The third resolution, an Amendment offered by Alexander Clark of Missouri, was approved:

"Resolved, that it is the sense of this Convention that the National Grand Lodge, should be dissolved, to the end that the system of Grand Lodge sovereignty may be better understood, and that peace and harmony may be restored."[23]

The third convention was held in Wilmington, Delaware, May 10, 1878, which in turn formed a "Grand Lodge Union" and issued thirteen resolutions and restrictions for its government. Number 10 being:

"And the Grand Lodges under the National Grand Lodge and the Independent Grand Lodges each solemnly pledge themselves to obey these articles, and we recommend that the National Grand Lodge do, when these articles are approved...wind up its affairs and adjourn *sine die*." ± =

**2.   Was the National Grand Lodge of North America dissolved?**

The following by Harry A. Williamson is of interest:

The American Masonic system requires that at least three Lodges are necessary for the formation of a Grand Lodge and while this writer is unaware of any regulation governing the formation of a national governing Masonic body with Grand Lodges subordinate to its mandates, it must be presumed that the same rules as to the number of grand bodies participating in the formation of such a body. The records reveal that at the meeting held on June 24, 1847, at Boston, *only two* Grand Lodges were represented, to wit: Boyer Grand Lodge of New York and Prince Hall Grand Lodge of Massachusetts and this fact was the cause of the adjournment of that Assembly and Prince Hall Grand Lodge engaged in a celebration of the Feast of St. John.

The representative of the First Independent African Grand Lodge of Pennsylvania did not reach Boston until June 25th, because the former held a similar celebration of the Feast of St. John in Philadelphia on June 24, 1847. Consequently, such records as have been examined state the Assembly reconvened on June 25th and held sessions on the 26th, 27th and 28th.

Sessions of the National Grand Lodge were held as follows:

New York City—October 13, 1848. June 25th to 29th, 1849 at Philadelphia, Pa.

1st Triennial—June 21st to 25th, 1850, place unknown.

2nd Triennial—July, 1853, place unknown. (Probably not held.)

2nd Triennial—March 31, 1854 at Philadelphia, Pa.

3rd Triennial—July 7th to 21st, 1856 at Philadelphia, Pa. (There is the date of 1858 but nothing else)

4th Triennial—August 4, 1859 at Cincinnati, Ohio and this was adjourned to July 4, 1860 at Pittsburgh, Pa.

5th Triennial—October 7th to 9th, 1862 at New York City.

6th Triennial—October 16th to 27th, 1865 at Baltimore, Md.

7th Triennial—October 5, 1868—place unknown. A meeting was held at Wilmington, Del., October 9, 1869.

8th Triennial—October 1871, at Chicago, Ill.

9th Triennial—May 11th to 15th at Louisville, Ky. 1874. A meeting was held under the call of Prince Hall Grand Lodge of Massachusetts at Boston, June 23rd and 24th, 1875.

10th Triennial—May 16th, 1877 at Pittsburgh, Pa. (This was the last regular meeting of record.)[26]

On September 4, 1877, representatives of 21 Jurisdictions met at Chicago, Ill.

A meeting was held at Wilmington, Del., in 1877, but the Grand Lodge therein had severed its connection with the National Grand Lodge and it has been claimed this was the real session of dissolution.

A notice was issued for a meeting to be held at Wilmington, Del., on May 8, 1878, but none was held.

Note: The proceedings of the Grand Lodge of Connecticut for the years 1874 and 1875, contains the statement that a meeting was held in the City of Philadelphia, Pa., at which time a majority of the representatives voted to dissolve the National Grand Lodge.

Richard H. Gleaves was the last National Grand Master of the National Grand Lodge and following the dissolution, he became the Fraternal Correspondent of the "Independent" Grand Lodge of the District of Columbia later known as the Acacia Grand Lodge but now known as the Prince Hall Grand Lodge F. & A.M. of the District of Columbia.

3. **When did the various Grand Lodges sever all connections with the National Grand Lodge?**

1. Prince Hall Grand Lodge of Mass., withdrew on December 18, 1873.

2. Pennsylvania

(a) Hiram Grand Lodge withdrew on November 9, 1849.

(b) The Independent or State Rights grand body denounced the Compact on June 28, 1850.

(c) The Compact unit and the Independent grand body consolidated into what is now Prince Hall Grand Lodge on the 24th day of December, 1882.

3. New York:

(a) Boyer Grand Lodge repudiated the signatures of its representatives to the Compact on June 7, 1848.

(b) Boyer Grand Lodge, after some of its dissenters had withdrawn from it, was re-organized October 13, 1848, under the title of the "United Grand Lodge."

(c) The "United Grand Lodge" and the Compact unit consolidated into what is now Prince Hall Grand Lodge on December 27, 1878.

4. Maryland:

The First Independent Colored Grand Lodge and the Union Grand Lodge (Compact) consolidated into what is now Prince Hall Grand Lodge of Maryland on September 12, 1876.

5. Missouri:

The Union Grand Lodge (National Compact) resolved into a State Rights or independent grand body July 31, 1871.

6. New Jersey:

(a) An independent or State Rights Grand Lodge was erected April 29, 1950.

(b) The Union Grand Lodge (Compact) and the independent grand body consolidated into what is now Prince Hall Grand Lodge, December 29, 1875.

7. Ohio:

This jurisdiction withdrew from the Compact on September 21, 1868, and is now known as Prince Hall Grand Lodge.

8. Delaware:

The independent or State Rights jurisdiction denounced the National Compact on July 1, 1850.

9. California:

The National Grand Lodge unit in the state and the Conventional Independent Grand Lodge consolidated into what is now Prince Hall Grand Lodge on June 24, 1874.

10. Indiana:

This jurisdiction severed it's connection with the National Grand Lodge on June 23, 1873.

11. Rhode Island:

Union Grand Lodge (Independent) and Harmony Grand Lodge (Compact) consolidated into what is now Prince Hall Grand Lodge on October 17, 1875.

12. Louisiana:

Eureka Grand Lodge (Independent) and Union Grand Lodge (Compact) consolidated into what is now Prince Hall Grand Lodge in 1874.

13. Michigan:

(a) The Compact unit dissolved September 22, 1873.

(b) Unity Grand Lodge (Independent) and the former members of the Compact body, consolidated into what is now Prince Hall Grand Lodge on September 23, 1873.

14. Virginia:

(a) Union Grand Lodge (Compact) was erected October 29, 1865.

(b) A State Rights or Independent grand body was erected October 14, 1867.

(c) The above named grand bodies consolidated into the present Grand Lodge on December 15, 1875.

15. Kentucky:

Ths jurisdiction withdrew from the National Grand Lodge in 1875.

16. Illinois:

This grand body withdrew from the Compact in 1875.

17. Kansas:

King Solomon Grand Lodge withdrew from the Compact and was re-organized into what is now Prince Hall Grand Lodge at a meeting held March 7th to 9th, 1876.

18. North Carolina:

This jurisdiction withdrew from the Compact during the year 1872, and is now Prince Hall Grand Lodge.

19. Florida:

The Independent or State Rights grand body and the Compact unit, consolidated into what is now "Union" Grand Lodge on June 12, 1872. [27]

20. Georgia:

(a) A unit of the National Grand Lodge was established August 22, 1870.

(b) An indepenent grand body was erected June 23, 1874.

(c) The foregoing jurisdictions consolidated into what is now Prince Hall Grand Lodge, in June, 1888.

21. Tennessee:

(a) An Independent jurisdiction was formed August 3, 1870.

(b) A National Compact unit was established September 19, 1871.

(c) The above bodies consolidated into what is now Prince Hall Grand Lodge on June 12, 1888.

22. Ontario: (Dominion of Canada)

This jurisdiction withdrew from the Compact during 1868, and is now known as Prince Hall Grand Lodge F. & A.M. of the Province of Ontario.

An examination of the foregoing facts, will reveal that 20 Grand Lodges severed their allegiance to the National Grand Lodge prior to the year 1877, and that the rival grand bodies in the several states had likewise consolidated into independent Grand Lodges for their respective areas.

Thus it is apparant that when the National Grand Lodge, (or such of it as was left) was scheduled to meet in Wilmington, Del., in 1877, there was nothing for the organization to do but dissolve, because, no Grand Lodges were represented to call a meeting.

In view of these facts, the claim that any group of gentlemen insist the National Grand Lodge did not dissolve, is positively fraudulent. [28]

# Notes for Part III

1. Albert Mackey: *Mackey's Revised Encyclopedia of Freemasonry,* Vol. 1 (New York, Macoy, 1956) pp. 389-399.

2. Ray V. Denslow: *The Masonic Conservators,* (Missouri, Grand Lodge A.F. & A.M., 1931).

3. To paraphrase Henry W. Coil: "Grand Masters and Grand Lodge Committees looked for analogies in the civil law more than they did for precedents in Masonic regulations. So, American (Mainstream) Freemasonry came under a new Masonic law modeled upon, and having all the rigidity of civil statutes and supported by sanction correspondingly severe. The lack of precedent or even of rationale of a rule did not retard its enforcement, though, on occasion when expediency dictated, the rules were qualified or ignored, Henry W. Coil, *Conversation on Freemasonry (Transactions of the Missouri Lodge of Research, Vol. 32, 1976)*

4. *Jno. G. Lewis, Jr.: End of an Era: History of the Prince Hall Grand Lodge of Louisiana 1848-1979.* By Joseph A. Walkes, Jr.

5. About the year 1859, Brother Rob Morris, a Freemason of some distinction in America, professed to have discovered by his researches, what he called the true Preston-Webb work, and attempted to introduce it into various Jurisdictions, sometimes in opposition to the wishes of White Grand Lodges and the leading Freemasons of the State. To aid in the propagation of this ritual he communicated it to several persons, who were bound to use all efforts to secure its adoption by their respective Grand Lodges. These Freemasons were called by him *Conservators,* and the order or society which they constituted was called the "Conservators Association." *Encyclopedia of Freemasonry,* Albert G. Mackey, (New York, Macoy, 1966) p. 238. For a fascinating study of this subject see, *The Masonic Conservators* by Ray V. Denslow (Missouri, Masonic Service Association, 1931)

The Grand Lodges of the United States of America from the commencement of the Revolutionary War began to abandon their dependence on the Grand Lodges of England and Scotland—that is to say, as soon as they emerged from the subordinate position of provincial Grand Lodges and were compelled to assume a sovereign and independent character, attempts have from time to time been made by members of the Craft to destroy this sovereignty of the State Grand Lodges, and to institute in its place a superintending power, to be constituted either as a Grand Master of North America or as a General Grand Lodge of the United States. Led, perhaps, by the analogy of the united colonies under one federal head or, in the very commencement of the Revolutionary struggle, controlled by long habits of dependence on the Mother Grand Lodges of Europe, the contest had no sooner begun, and a disserverance of political relations between England and America taken place, than the attempt was made to institute the office of Grand Master of the United States, the object being (of which there can hardly be a doubt) to invest [George] Washington with the distinguished dignity. *Encyclopedia of Freemasonry*, Albert G. Mackey (New York, Macoy, 1966) p. 389.

6. *Ibid*

7. Paper, *A History of the Most Worshipful National Grand Lodge*, author unknown, though, it is believed to be Harold Van Buren Voorhis. Author's collection.

8. *Address to the Colored Masonic Fraternity of the United States*, by William T. Boyd, *Proceedings* of the Prince Hall Grand Lodge of Ohio, 1871, p. 87.

9. Boyd writes that Massachusetts "never had or ever could have, except by assumption, the show of a title to the name of a Grand Lodge. We mean, and we speak advisedly, the so-called and self-styled "African Grand Lodge of Massachusetts." And we now assert and challenge the proof to the contrary, that she never had any power beyond that of the Master Mason's Lodge." Boyd continues that:

> "Certain members of the present colored Grand Lodge of Massachusetts, in their petition to the white Grand Lodge of that State for recognition, say that the colored Grand Lodge was formed in 1808, by one Lodge in Boston, one in Providence and one in Philadelphia, that these, under Prince Hall, organized a Grand Lodge in Boston. This may be so.

> "But how is it that no proofs of the fact are brought forward, and that the best informed members of the fraternity in Philadelphia and New York had no knowledge of it in 1847 and 1849, when they put forth the declaration that there was no Grand Lodge in Massachusetts, and little or no fraternal relations between the Masons of different places, and members of different Lodges in the same place." *Ibid*, p. 89.

10. *Ibid*, p. 89

11. *New Regulations: VIII.* Every Brother concerned in making Masons clandestinely, shall be allowed, to visit any Lodge till he had made due submission, even tho' the Brother so admitted may be allowed. None who make a stated Lodge without the Grand Master's Warrant, shall be admitted into regular Lodges, till they make due submission and obtain grace. If any Brethren form a Lodge without leave, and shall irregulary make new Brothers, they shall not be admitted into any regular Lodge, no not as visitors, till they render a good reason, or make due submission.

*Old Regulations: VIII...*if any set or number of Masons, shall take upon themselves to form a Lodge without the Grand Master's Warrant, the regular Lodges are not to countenance them, nor own them as fair Brethren duly formed, nor approve of their acts and deeds, but must treat them as Rebels, until they humble themselves as the Grand Master shall in his Prudence direct, and until he approve of them by his Warrant signified to the other Lodges, as the Custom is when a new Lodge is to be registered in the Grand Lodge Book. (Lawrence Dermott: *Ahiman Rezon,* a facsimile reprint of the first edition of 1756, (Illinois, Masonic Book Club, 1972) pp. 57-58.

12. *Proceedings* of the Sixth Triennial Session of the Most Worshipful National Grand Lodge of Free and Accepted Ancient York Masons of the United States of North America. Held in the City of Baltimore, October A.D. 1865-A.L. 5865 (Philadelphia, D.E. Thomas Printers, 1866) pp. 63-64.

13. Aldrage B. Cooper, *Footprints of Prince Hall Masonry in New Jersey* (New York, Henry Emmerson Press, 1957) p. 4.

14. A.G. Clark, *The National Grand Lodge: Sketch of its History, Workings and Dissolution* (Most Worshipful United (Prince Hall) Grand Lodge of Iowa, 1921) p. 9.

15. *Proceedings* of the Sixth Triennial Session, 1865, p. 65.

16. Cooper: *op cit.,* pp. 5-6.

17. *Proceedings* of the Sixth Triennial Session, 1865, p. 8.

18. Harry E. Davis, *Freemasonry Among Negroes in America* (United Supreme Council, A.A.S.R., Northern Jurisdiction, PHA., 1946) p. 102.

19. Boyd, *Ibid.*

20. *Proceedings* Prince Hall Grand Lodge of Ohio, 1878, pp. 27 & 66.

21. Grand Lodges of the States of Alabama, Arkansas, Georgia, Illinois, Kansas, Kentucky, Louisiana, Michigan, Missouri, Ohio, Ontario, Pennsylvania and Rhode Island; two sets of representatives from Kansas and Michigan. *Proceedings* of Prince Hall Grand Lodge of Missouri, 1877. *Supplemental Appendix* p. 149.

22. *Ibid.*

23. *Ibid.*

24. *Proceedings* Prince Hall Grand Lodge of Ohio, 1878, p. 65; *Proceedings* Prince Hall Grand Lodge of Missouri, 1877, *Supplemental Appendix*, p. 140.

25. *Proceedings* Prince Hall Grand Lodge of Ohio, 1878, pp. 27-29.

26. The *Proceedings* of the Grand Lodge of Connecticut for the years 1874 and 1875 contains the statement that a meeting was held in the City of Philadelphia at which time a majority of the representatives voted to dissolve the National Grand Lodge.

27. There is a so-called Grand Lodge operating within Florida which styles itself as Prince Hall Grand Lodge but it is not recognized by the Prince Hall Fraternity.

About the year 1910, a schism arose in the Union Grand Lodge and a group of lodges together with numerous individual Masons, withdrew from the Mother Grand Lodge and established this so-called Prince Hall Jurisdiction and became incorporated under that title. For many years it has been closely associated with a group which is styled as "bogus" by the Prince Hall Fraternity.

28. Harry A. Williamson, *Facts About the Dissolution of the National Grand Lodge of North America.* (author's collection.)

For a different viewpoint see John M. Sherman: *The Negro "National" or "Compact" Grand Lodges, Ars Quatuor Coronatorum, Vol. 92, 1979*, pp. 148-171. Sherman's paper seems more of an intent to attack Prince Hall Freemasonry in a one-sided paper that goes nowhere.

# PART FOUR

# The Damning of Saint Orgne

This chapter title is taken from an article "The Revelation of Saint Orgne the Damned" by W. E. B. DuBois in *Fisk News* 11 (November-December, 1938, pp. 3-9) and reprinted in 1939 as a sixteen page pamphlet. The cryptic title becomes clearer when it is realized that Orgne means Negro.

1.  **How does Prince Hall Freemasonry view its counterparts of mainstream American Masonry?**

    The following, taken from mainsteam Freemasonry, will help answer the above question.

    (1) Grand Lodge, A.F. & A.M. of Iowa, *Proceedings* for 1852:

    "Exclusion of persons of the Negro race is in accordance with Masonic law and the ancient Charges and Regulations."

    (2) Grand Lodge, F. & A.M. of Louisiana, decision of the Grand Master, 1924:

    "A mixture of white and Negro blood made a man ineligible for the degrees of Masonry."[1]

    (3) Grand Lodge, A.F. & A.M. of North Carolina, Constitution, edition of 1915, Section 110, page 50:

    "A candidate "must be a free-born white man."

    (4) Grand Ldoge, F. & A.M. of Mississippi, (a) *Proceedings* for 1899, page 43, and (b) Constitution of Grand Lodge, edition of 1914, states:

    "A Mason who discusses Freemasonry with a Negro should be expelled from his Lodge."

(5) Grand Lodge, F. & A.M. of Ohio, *Proceedings* for 1847:
"Admission of persons of color should be inexpedient and tend to mar the harmony of the fraternity."

(6) Grand Lodge, A.F. & A.M. of Idaho, *Proceedings* for 1916, page 16:
Decision of Francis Jenkins, Grand Master: "Ruled that a candidate "must be a white man." This decision was approved by the Committee on Masonic Jurisprudence.

(7) Grand Lodge, A.F.M. of South Carolina. The "Ahiman Rezon" compiled by Albert G. Mackey, Grand Secretary, says:
"...that a candidate must be of free white parents."

(8) Grand Lodge, F. & A.M. of New York, (a) *Proceedings* for 1851:
"I. It is not proper to initiate in our Lodges, persons of the Negro race; and their exclusion is in accordance with Masonic law and the Ancient Charges, and regulations, because of their depressed social condition; the general lack of intelligence, which unfit them, as a body, to work or adorn the craft; the impropriety in making them our equals in one place, when from their social condition, and the circumstances which almost everyone attach to them, we cannot do so in others, their not being, as a general thing FREE BORN; the impossibility, or at least the difficulty of ascertaining, if we once commence, their free birth, and where the line of intelligence and social elevation commences and ends, or divide portions of race; finally, their not being, as a race, persons of 'good report,' or who can be 'well recommended' as subjects for initiation; they very seldom being persons who have any trade, estate, office, occupation, or visible way of acquiring an honest livelihood, and working in the craft, as becomes members of this ancient and honorable fraternity, but likewise something to spare for the works of charity, and for supporting the ancient grandeur and dignity of the Royal Craft; 'eating no man's bread for naught,' and their general positive deficiency of natural endowments."

(b) *Proceedings* for 1890: "That to initiate Negroes into Lodges would disrupt the Fraternity throughout the country."

(9) Grand Lodge, F. & A.M. of Kentucky

(a) *Proceedings* for 1914, page 39:

"A man possessing one-eighth to one-sixteenth degree of Negro blood cannot be made a Mason."

(b) The Constitution, edition of 1919, page 28:

"A candidate must be a free-born white man."

(c) *Proceedings* for 1947, page 139, the Secretary of Lodge No. 228, asked, "Can a Catholic join the Masons?" The decision of Albert C. Hanson, Grand Master, in Opinion No. 45, stated: "Sec. 105, Book of Constitutions states a candidate for initiation must be a free-born white man, of the age of twenty-one or more and of good report."

(10) Grand Lodge, A.F. & A.M. of Texas, Constitution and Laws, 1948, Article XV, page 34:

"This Grand Lodge does not recognize as legal or Masonic any body of Negroes working under any character of charter in the United States, without regard to the body granting such charter, and they regard all Negro lodges as clandestine, illegal and un-Masonic, and moreover, they regard as highly censurable the course of any Grand Lodge in the United States which shall recognize such bodies of Negroes as Masonic Lodges."

(11) Grand Lodge, A.F. & A.M. of Delaware, *Proceedings* for 1867:

A portion of the Obligation in the degree of Master Mason stated that the initiation or visitation:

"...of any Negro, mulatto, or colored person of the United States is forbidden."

(12) Grand Lodge, A.F. & A.M. of Illinois

(a) *Proceedings* for 1851:

A resolution was adopted forbidding either the initiation or visitation of a Negro in any lodge.

(b) *Proceedings* for 1852:

"...that this Grand Lodge is inqualifiedly opposed to the admission of Negroes or mulattoes into Lodges under this Jurisdiction."[2]

(c) *Proceedings* for 1899:

"Therefore to have Lodges exclusively of Negroes, would be dangerous to the high character of our Order. And, to associate them in Lodges with white brethren, would be impossible."

(13) Grand Lodge, F. & A.M. of Mississippi

(a) *Proceedings* for 1909:

A candidate was denied advancement in his lodge because he had been instructed in his previous degree by a Negro.

(b) *Proceedings* for 1914:

Because he did not know it was wrong and so explained to the lodge, that he had visited a lodge of Negroes in ignorance, a member of Lodge No. 34, was acquitted of any wrong doing.

Because of the acquittal, the Grand Master arrested the Charter of the Lodge; he stated the member should have been punished.

(14) Grand Lodge, A.F. & A.M. of Illinois

(a) *Proceedings* for 1846:

The Master of a lodge was punished because he had conferred the degrees upon a gentleman whose mother had been a Cherokee Indian and his father a mulatto.

(b) *Proceedings* for 1852 (?):

"The Grand Lodge of Illinois reproved one of its subordinates for admitting a half-blooded American Indian as a visitor, and passed a resolution prohibiting, under severe penalty, a repetition of such offense."[3]

(c) *Proceedings* for 1912:

A Past Master of a lodge, together with a Past Senior Warden and another member, assisted as pallbearers at the funeral of a Negro Mason. The Past Master was expelled from his lodge and the two others were suspended for one year.

(15) Grand Lodge, F. & A.M. of New York

*Proceedings* for 1851:

A resolution was adopted declaring that men of the Indian race in America were unfit material for Masonry.

Although there is no record extant as to when that prohibition was removed, the jurisdiciton has, for many years, openly boasted about certain prominent members of the Indian race who have been made Masons in its lodges.

(16) Grand Lodge, F. & A.M. of Indiana, *Proceedings* for 1945:

The Grand Master of the Grand Lodge refused to permit the initiation of a gentleman of Chinese birth upon the ground that he was not a citizen of the United States.

(17) Grand Lodge, A.F. & A.M. of Province of Quebec (Dominion of Canada)

(a) *Proceedings* for 1923:

Charles McBurney, Grand Master, informed his Grand Lodge that he had refused permission to a group of Negroes who wished to establish a lodge in the city of Montreal.

(b) *Proceedings* for 1927:

William J. Ewing, Grand Master, refused to grant permission to a group of Negroes to erect a lodge in Montreal.

(18) Grand Lodge, A.F. & A.M. of Texas

Constitution, edition of 1876: Article XXXVI, declared that all lodges of Negroes were clandestine and illegal.

(19) Grand Lodge, F. & A.M. of Mississippi

(a) *Proceedings* for February 9, 1899:

Because the Grand Lodge of Washington had declared that if Negroes established lodges and in time a Grand Lodge in that State, the former would not consider such to be an invasion of its Masonic territory, the Grand Lodge of Mississippi severed fraternal relations with the Grand Lodge of Washington.

(b) *Proceedings* for 1873:

Although the Grand Master, W.H. Hardy, advised his Grand Lodge that one in New Jersey had permitted the formation of a lodge at Newark, N.J., whose membership consisted of both whites and blacks, the Mississippi grand body took no action at that time, but it did about 1909.

(c) *Proceedings* for 1909:

During the Month of August, 1908, Edwin J. Martin, Grand Master, discovered that Alpha Lodge, No. 116, working under the white Grand Lodge of New Jersey in the city of Newark, had a membership comprising both whites and blacks and because the Grand Master of New Jersey would not disown the Lodge, the Grand Master of Mississippi declared relations between his and the New Jersey grand body at an end.[4]

(20) Grand Lodge, A.F. & A.M. of Oklahoma

(a) *Proceedings* for February 9, 1910:

Because of its sympathy with the action of the Grand Master of Mississippi as just referred to, this Grand Lodge severed relations with the Grand Lodge of New Jersey because of racial composition of Alpha Lodge, No. 116, under the jurisdiction of the latter.

Later, Oklahoma resumed relations with the understanding that all Masons from New Jersey would be welcomed into the Oklahoma lodges except those members of Alpha Lodge, No. 116.

(b) *Proceedings* for February 14, 1940:

The Grand Lodge of Oklahoma again discovered the existence of Alpha Lodge No. 116, at Newark, and again severed fraternal relations with the Grand Lodge of New Jersey but these were resumed again on February 11, 1942.

(21) Arizona Lodge, No. 2, F. & A.M. at Phoenix, Arizona:

Under the date of January 5, 1952, the Associated Press sent out a news dispatch telling that the body of a Negro soldier, who had been killed in Korea, had been held in a mortuary in the city of Phoenix *for five weeks* because the cemetery owned and operated by Arizona Lodge No. 2, would not permit the body to be buried therein unless three notarized letters of request for burial were submitted from as many veteran organizations to bury the remains of PFC Thomas C. Reed beside those of white veterans in the cemetery of that Masonic Lodge.

This cemetery which is maintained by that Masonic Lodge is the only non-Catholic cemetery in that city in which a Negro can be buried and even then it has a special and separate section for Negroes, Chinese and Japanese so as to keep their remains away from those of the whites.

Private Reed's body had already awaited burial for five weeks, and many days elapsed following the spreading of the news of the action of that Masonic Lodge before a permit could be obtained to have the remains of the Negro solider buried.[5]

2.  **The above events took place many many years ago. Does it serve any purpose to record them in 1983?**

In order to answer the question raised in item No. 1 there must be a full realization of the events in American Freemasonry which have taken place.

To continue:

(1)   General Albert Pike:

This gentlemen has been credited with having developed the system of the Ancient and Accepted Scottish Rite of Freemasonry to its present high standing in America, becoming its most outstanding proponent and the author of that voluminous work pertaining to the Rite bearing the title of *Morals and Dogma.*

He was born in Massachusetts where there was relatively little outward expression of race and color prejudice in comparison to other sections of the country. Later, he removed to Arkansas where he apparently readily absorbed much of the race prejudice which prevailed thereabouts.

This gentleman very readily admitted as his opinion that the Prince Hall Fraternity was just as regular as his own and in some instances, more so, but he was unable to overcome the matter of color as expressed in the following language:

"I took my obligations to white men, not Negroes. When I have to accept Negroes as Brethern or leave Masonry, I shall leave it."[6]

(2) Fredrick Speed was the Grand Secretary of the Grand Lodge of Mississippi and he wrote an article for his newspaper which read as follows:

"But Scipie Africanus is simple but a brute, with no revenge or resentments, and no respect for the truth or purity of his woman. Whiskey and cocaine and miscognation are his bane and until some remedy is found for these great evils, the poor fellow will continue to go down lower and lower in the social scale until finally the time will come when he and white man must part company."[7]

(3) A Mason who belonged to a Grand Lodge in the northern section wrote in 1890:

"We know that Masonry is not only close in fellowship, but it is perfect in morals, and intricate in science. And we know that the Negroes of the South are wholly incompetent to embrace it. They are ignorant, immoral, untruthful, and, intellectually, they are more impotent than minority or dotage—both of which we exclude. It would be very rare if any locality could furnish the requisite number of sufficient capacity to open a Lodge. Therefore, to have Lodges exclusively of Negroes would be dangerous to the high character of our Order. And, to associate them with white brethren would be impossible."[8]

(4) In commenting upon some remarks appearing in the Proceedings of an American Grand Lodge, the Fraternal Correspondent of the Grand Lodge of Western Australian wrote as follows:

"The magnitude of the 'color question' is far too great for more than passing reference in this review. At the same time, the writer feels that no man, whether white or colored, who is 'totally, morally, and intellectually incapacitated' is qualified to enter our ranks. Do the Past Grand Master and committee (of Mississippi) wish to leave the impression that every colored man is, for the reasons quoted, disqualified. If so, will they ask themselves the question: Are there no good colored men wearing a colored skin, and are the colored folk creatures of another Creator than God whom we, as Masons, acknowledge?"[9]

The reply to the above query reads:

"Now, to a Brother in Western Australia, and equally to one in Maine, no doubt it is natural that a Negro seems to be simply a black white man, with like impulses and instincts, who, under like auspices, would have like moral sense and similiar, if not identical, reasoning powers. No arguments we (who have known them well for a lifetime, as free and slave) could advance, would change their fixed views, but how utterly wrong they are in their disregard of scientific ethnology. No Negro ever born is the social or moral peer of a white man...To return to the question above, we will say 'the colored folk' are the creatures of the same Creator as ourselves, but so are Kentucky mules. The Negroes have many good traits, but they cannot make Masons any more than they would make good husbands for our daughters."[10]

In commenting upon the above reply, Louis Block, Fraternal Correspondent of the Grand Lodge of Iowa wrote:

"While we are a northerner, Bro. Eggleston, still we are in hearty accord with you on this subject."[11]

Today, in 1983, in various quarters across the United States there has been seen a change of heart and effort has been made by mainstream Freemasonry to meet the Prince Hall Fraternity on the "square." It is true there are many Freemasons who are known to be genuinely sympathetic to the aims and aspirations of the Prince Hall order. This can be seen by the publication of this work by a Caucasian Masonic body, but, unfortunately, these events do not make a dent in the antagonistic attitude displayed by the majority of mainstream Grand Lodges against Prince Hall Freemasonry. What is recorded above, is but the tip of the iceberg, and volumes upon volumes could be filled on the relationship of Mainstream Amercian Freemasonry and Prince Hall Freemasonry. Without a doubt one will not be free until the other is free, for we are tied one to the other, by the mere fact that we are American citizens, and we share a common ground.

Some years ago, a Civil Rights leader noted that "the Church was the most segregated institution in America," but he was mistaken. Freemasonry is the most segregated institution in America, and this to its shame. Mainstream American Freemasory and Prince Hall Freemasonry must come together under the true Fatherhood of God and the Brotherhood of Man with the respect that is due God's creatures, or Freemasonry in America is doomed!

## Notes for Part Four

1. The *Square & Compass*, New Orleans, La., August 24, 1924, cited by Harry A. Williamson, "Anti-Negro Masonic Legislation in American Masonry," (authors collection).

2. The *Freemason's Monthly Magazine*, Boston, Mass., July 1853, page 287, cited by Williamson *ibid.* See also Vol. VII, No. 2, 2nd Quarter 1981 issue of the *Phylaxis* magazine, pp. 33-34 Editorial: The Phylaxis and Cerza's "Prince Hall Organization," for reproduction of page from the *Proceedings* of the Grand Lodge A.F.& A.M. of Illionis.

3. The *Freemasons Monthly Magazine*, Boston, Mass., July 1853, cited by Williamson, *ibid.*

4. *Harold V.B. Voorhis, Negro Masonry in the United States*, (New York, Henry Emmerson, 1949) pp. 100/102 cited by Wiliamson, ibid. It is interesting to note that as late as 1947, Texas *Proceedings* reported under its committee on Foreign Correspondence, dated December 3rd, remarks of R. Bruce Brannon, Grand Master, who refers to Article XV, of the Constitution and Laws of the Grand Lodge that:

"I suppose it is wholly unnecessary for me to point out that it is the law of our Grand Lodge that the Grand Lodge of Texas does not recognize as legal or Masonic any body of Negroes working under any character of charter in the United States without regard to the body granting such charter, and that this Grand Lodge regards all Negro Lodges as clandestine, illegal and un-Masonic and this Grand Lodge regards as highly censurable the course of any Grand Lodge in the United States which shall recognize such bodies of Negroes as Masons."

Therefore, this would mean that although the Grand Lodge of Texas recognizes the White Grand Lodge of New Jersey, a censure of that grand body is implied over the existence of Alpha Lodge, No. 116.

From time to time, this writer has received letters from members of Alpha Lodge No. 116, bitterly complaining of the treatment they receive at the hands of Prince Hall Freemasons, who treat them as clandestine. My standard reply is: there is no reason for a Alpha Lodge No. 116 so long as there is a Prince Hall Grand Lodge of New Jersey. They are treated like second class citizens when they travel outside of the State of New Jersey. Mainstream Freemasonry doesn't want them, and Prince Hall Freemasonry rejects them! Also, over the years, I have received letters from maintream members of the Craft stating that they attended communications with Alpha Lodge with none expressing that sitting in Lodge with Blacks was a "fraternal experience" but rather a curiosity.

5. The *New York Times*, New York City, January 6 1952, cited by Williamson, *ibid.*

6. *"Light on a Dark Subject"* by William H. Upton (Prince Hall Grand Lodge of Mass., 1902) pp. 214-215. Albert Pike served as Chief Justice of the Ku Klux Klan at the time he was Sovereign Grand Commander. He was also Grand Dragon for Arkansas cited in the *Phylaxis*, Vol. VIII, No.1, 1st Quarter 1982 *"The Ku Klux Klan and Regular Freemasonry"* by Joseph A. Walkes, Jr., FPS, pp. 3-8.

7. The *Southland*, Vicksburg, Miss, April 24, 1909, cited by Harry A. Williamson *"Anti-Negro Expressions in American Freemasonry."* (authors collection).

8. *Proceedings of Grand Lodge of Virginia, 1913,* Appendix, page 59, cited by Williamson, ibid.

9. *Proceedings* of Grand Lodge of Virginia, 1913, Appendix, page 59, cited by Williamson, *ibid.*

10. *op cit.*

11. *op cit.*

NOTE: The following written by Harry A. Williamson is of interest:

### The Present Attitude of American Masonry
### toward the
### Prince Hall Fraternity

It appears that rumors have been circulated in various quarters to the effect that the American Masons have undergone a great change of heart and have developed what has been characterized as a "good feeling" toward the Prince Hall Fraternity.

It is true there are many Freemasons who are known to be genuinely sympathetic to the aims and aspirations of the Prince Hall Order, but, unfortunately, these are either in the minority in their jurisdictions or not in stations of influence in their respective areas, while, on the other hand it is equally true there are those who are rabidly antagonistic; these represent the majority in their grand bodies and the records will reveal, in no uncertain language, the measure of their race hatred.

Not unlike the Washington craft in 1898, the Grand Lodge of Massachusetts in 1947, adopted a report submitted by a committee of Past Grand Masters which had instituted an investigation of the status of Prince Hall Masonry in that state.

The reaction of a large number of Grand Lodges as similar to that in 1898 and 1899, in the Washington incidents, with the exception, there was less personal invective hurled at the Massachusetts committee, than to the one in Washington. A great amount of personal abuse was heaped upon William H. Upton, chairman of the Washington committee and even the death of his wife about that time did not soften those invectives from some quarters.

It is not necessary to quote the entire Washington committee report, but several excerpts will be presented to illustrate how close the 1947 action of Massachusetts was to that of Washington in 1898;...so the parallel from Massachusetts is as follows:

> There is a need for unifying and strengthening all influences for the improvement and uplifting of mankind. Freemasonry seeks to build character and promote brotherhood among all men. These objectives have nothing to do with race or color or social or economic status. In this country, the welfare and the future of the white and colored people are interdependent and largely identical. Each has its own schoools and colleges and churches and societies, but both have the same ultimate hopes and aspirations; both make common sacrifices in defense of their single country; both read the same periodicals, hear the same radio programs, and enjoy or suffer together the triumphs or failures of our national well being; and each is affected by the material and spiritual welfare of the other.
>
> *In conclusion, your Committee believes that in view of the existing social conditions in our country, it is advisable for the official and organized activities of white and colored Freemasons to proceed in paralled lines, but organically separate and without mutually embarrassing demands or commitments.*

*However, your Committee believes that, within these limita-
tions, informal cooperation and mutual helpfulness between the
two groups upon appropriate occasions are desirable.*
*(Williamson's Italics)*

In the statement of the chairman of the Massachusetts committee,
reference was made to Melvin M. Johnson, P.G.M., and a member of
the committee, there appeared this language:

> "He first called attention to the fact that the Committee *does
> not* recommend what is technically known Masonically as
> '*recognition.*' *Neither does it recommend intervisitation. Mere
> acknowledgement of legitimacy implies neither.*"

Noting the widespread unfavorable reaction of some of the Masons
who have no doubt boasted about the Fatherhood of God and the
Brotherhood of Man, it is very apparent they had no intention
whatever of respecting the sincerity of the statement above quoted.
With many, race prejudice was much deeper in their minds than were
the precepts of the Institution, and all took refuge behind the fallacy of
"exclusive territorial Jurisdiction," a claim which has never had any
fundamental status in Freemasonry at any time, anywhere.

In the following list are a few of the American grand bodies which
criticized Massachusetts, for its actions and these no doubt represent
the "good feeling" they have for the society of Freemasons of color:

> California—1947; California—1948; North Carolina—1947;
> Wisconsin—1948; District of Columbia—1947;
> Tennessee—1948; Nebraska—1948; Missouri—1946

Texas—1948: The following has been transcribed from the report of
Foreign Correspondence dated December 1st:

> "That the Grand Lodge of Texas discontinue all fraternal
> relations with the Most Worshipful Grand Lodge of
> Massachusetts. We hope in time the Most Worshipful Grand
> Lodge of Massachusetts *will see fit to recognize and
> acknowledge the rights of the Grand Lodge of Texas.*"
*(Williamson's Italics)*

Iowa—1949; Louisiana—1949: Resolution N. 14, begins on page
143 and continues to page 145, and of that document only the following are submitted:

> WHEREAS, the action of the Grand Lodge of Massachusetts
> has undermined, ignored and directly conflicted with the comi-
> ty that prevails among all regular Grand Lodges in the United
> States; and,

WHEREAS, the Grand Lodge of Massachusetts has disregarded the protest of the Grand Lodge of Texas and its duly appointed Committee on Foreign Correspondence; and,

WHEREAS, the Grand Lodge of Texas did as of December 1, 1948, discontinue all fraternal relations with the Most Worshipful Grand Lodge of Massachusetts; and,

WHEREAS, the Grand Lodge of Massachusetts has disregarded and ignored the protest and repudiation of the Grand Lodge of Louisiana, and its committee on Foreign correspondence registered at the Annual Communication of February, 1948;

THEREFORE, BE IT RESOLVED, at its Annual Communication that the Grand Lodge of the State of Louisiana, F.& A.M. discontinue all fraternal relations with the Most Worshipful Grand Lodge of Massachusetts. We hope in time the Most Worshipful Grand Lodge of Massachusetts will see fit to recognize and acknowledge the rights of the Grand Lodge of the State of Louisiana.

According to page 218 and 219 of the Louisiana *Proceedings*, a vote did not completely register the sentiment of the Grand Lodge so a substitute motion that action be deferred until the 1949 session prevailed by vote of 355 yeas vs 167 Nays.

Michigan—1949.

Some of the Masonic periodicals carried articles pertaining to the 1947 action, but it is unnecessary to submit a list of these and their reactions, because the latter is thoroughly understood.

However, the one periodical which has, over the years, been disrespectful to both the Negro race and its Masonic Order, has been *the New Age Magazine*, the official journal of the Supreme Council of the Southern Jurisdiction of the Scottish Rite. I have a record of issues of this magazine from about 1904 to and including 1950, in which editorials and contributions have breathed the spirit of race hatred in its truest sense. I must add, however, there are many members of the Jurisdiction who do not approve of the policy of the Magazine but they are unable to cause a change therein. That will rest solely, in my opinion, when the Grand Architect of the Universe shall place His finger on each one responsible.

It might prove to be of much interest for Prince Hall Masons to examine the following issues of this periodical.

| | |
|---|---|
| March—1947, p. 145 | January—1949, p. 22 |
| April—1948, p. 234 | April—1950, p. 212 |
| August—1948, p. 471 | |

As an illustration of the character of editorials which have appeared in *The New Age Magazine,* under the caption of "Some Phases of Race Problem," the following can be found on page 266, in the issue for May, 1949:

> "Let us call attention to verse 26, chapter 17, The Acts of the Apostles: 'And hath made of one blood all nations of men for to dwell on all the face of the earth, and hath determined the times before appointed, and the bounds of the habitation.'
>
> If the Great Architect of the Universe, by whatever name He may be called, wanted the red, brown, yellow, black and white races to be equal in every respect, he certainly would have started them that way in the beginning and would not have placed 'the bounds of their habitation,' *Some people misinterpret the first part of the verse, 'has made of one blood all nations.' for that means human blood as different from animal blood and that of other creatures."*

*(Williamsons Italics)*

The staid and highly respected Grand Lodge of Massachusetts could not withstand the great amount of pressure which was imposed upon it, and as great as that body was, it was compelled to disapprove its 1947 action in the following language, in part, in 1949:

> "Misunderstandings and statements which we feel to be erroneous have produced unfortunate events. *The net result is producing disharmony in American Freemasonry, whereas unity is what we need more than anything else. Unity and harmony are vastly more important to the Fraternity than debates about Negro Freemasonry."*

*(Williamson's Italics)*

There is no mistaking the meaning of the language appearing in the last sentence of the above quotation.

The only redeeming thing about the rescinding of its 1947 action was, the statement, as above, did not repudiate the sources nor the accuracy of the data upon which the committee of Past Grand Masters had based their findings.

It is interesting to note that John M. Sherman of the Grand Lodge of Massachusetts mentions the above rescission but fails to mention the real cause, in his review of *Prince Hall: Life and Legacy* by Charles H. Wesley in *Ars Quatuor Coroatorum,* Vol. 90, 1977, p. 310. He also fails to mention "An Open Letter to Members of the Grand Lodge of

Massachusetts, A.F. & A.M." dated October 31, 1969, which read in part:

"The 1949 committee report concluded with the pusillanimous decision that unity and harmony are vastly more important to the Fraternity then debates about Negro Freemasonry.

This statement, questionable then; today, is clearly untrue.

The Prince Hall Grand Lodge of Massachusetts recently has asked for the reaffirmation by your Grand Lodge of its own regularity and legitimacy, which so far as we are aware has never been questioned by any competent Masonic authority, and to share with you, by mutual consent, territorial jurisdiction within the commonwealth, as is specifically provided for in your own Constitutions.

Indeed, as M.W. Melvin M. Johnson pointed out in 1946, you have in fact shared this jurisdiction "for a century and a half" by that silence which tacitly gives consent.

In 1947, the Grand Lodge had the courage and the moral conviction to do what was right rather than what was most expedient. Since 1949 it has remained intimidated, lacking the wisdom to realize that what is righteous and just will survive any storm, whereas that which is expedient and unjust will not endure.

To continue to sweep the matter under the carpet where it will not have to be faced is inconsistent with the basic precepts of our institutuion. If we persist in doing so, inevitably we shall see Masonry diminishing in stature, becoming less and less meaningful, and eventually reaching a point where it will no longer have any justification for existence.

We urge all Massachusetts Masons to look into their hearts and consciences, to realize that nothing is ever settled until it is settled honestly and justly, and then to make their opinions upon the all important matter known to their own Lodges and to the Grand Master, as he has invited them to do. Let us remember that all that is necesary for injustice to prevail is that good men do nothing.

In compliance with the September 11, 1969 request of the Grand Master, this open letter is not sponsored by any Lodge as a group but by the following Massachusetts Masons as individuals.

Lewis P. Aronson
Presiding Master, Shawmut
Lodge, Boston

Louis S. Blackstone
Past Master, Shawmut Lodge

Erwin D. Canham
Editor in Chief, *The Christian Science Monitor*

Albert I. Green
Marshall, Shawmut Lodge

Stephen Green
Past Master, Shawmut Lodge

William L. Greene
Past Master, Shawmut Lodge

Marril I. Hassenfield
Senior Warden, Shawmut
Lodge

Halsey DeW. Howe
Chaplain, Lodge of St.
Andrew, Boston

John A. Jeffries, Jr.
Senior Warden, Lodge of St.
Andrew

Bernard Kalman
Past Master, Shawmut Lodge

Kivie Kaplain
President, National Association
for the Advancement of
Colored People

Bertram Martinson
Senior Steward, Shawmut
Lodge

Donald A. Moors
Past Master, Pittsfield Lodge,
Pittsfield

George M. Naylor, Jr.
Past Master, Lodge of St.
Andrew

William B. Osgood
Junior Warden, Lodge of St.
Andrew

Ben G. Shapiro
Commissioner, Massachusetts
Commission Against Discrimination

Albert M. Simmon
Past Master, Temple Lodge,
Boston

Harold L. Suvalle
Junior Deacon, Shawmut
Lodge

Edward Trachtenberg
Senior Deacon, Shawmut
Lodge

Winthrop Wetherbee, M.D.
Past Master, Lodge of St.
Andrew

# PART FIVE

# Of The Craft and Things

1. What was the approximate membership of Prince Hall Freemasonry in 1983?

   According to the figures released by the N.A.A.C.P. Prince Hall Masons Legal Research Department, there are approximately 4,675 lodges with a membership of 288,303. However, the Phylaxis Society, a research organization within Prince Hall Freemasonry, rounds the figures off at 5,000 Lodges and 300,000 members.

2. As to charity, what does Prince Hall Freemasonry support?

   Prince Hall Freemasonry supports basically those charities that assist the Black community. It has been extensive over the years. Though figures are not ususally compiled on its contributions, the Prince Hall Conference of Grand Masters list $949,038 to the N.A.A.C.P. Legal Defense Fund alone. In 1982 the United Supreme Council 33°, A.A.S.R, Southern Jurisdiction PHA contributed $100,000 to Black institutions of higher learning across the country, and each Grand Lodge contributes yearly to the N.A.A.C.P., Urban League, United Negro Fund, O.I.C., and various other civil rights organizations. The Prince Hall Shrine annual grants to the Prince Hall Shrine Health and Medical Research Foundation, formerly known as the T.B. and Cancer Research Foundation, is in the thousands of dollars. There are annual grants of $6,000 each to several institutions of higher learning and to hospitals. A national scholarship grant program for young ladies between the ages of 17—24 to attend colleges and universities of their choice, as well as a $20,000 annual grant for special scholarships for economically deprived youths, as well as a program of finacial aid to youths in the inner city in the fight against drugs, crimes and delinquency in the streets. All in all, Prince Hall Freemasonry does a most commendable job in its charitable programs.

3. **Has the name "African" been perpetuated?**

The only Lodge this writer is aware of is "African Four-Fifty Nine" No. 63 of Brooklyn, New York. However there have been at least two others, but they are now extinct.

4. **Have there been any Prince Hall lodges named after William H. Upton, P.G.M. of the mainstream Grand Lodge of the State of Washington, and author of *Negro Masonry*?**

The Prince Hall Grand Lodge of the State of Washington has William H. Upton Lodge No. 11 at Walla Walla and the Prince Hall Grand Lodge of South Carolina has William H. Upton Lodge No. 145 at Richburg, S.C.

5. **Has any lodge been named for a Black who was a native of a foreign country?**

L'Overture Lodge No. 156 at Richmond, Virginia is named for the hero of the Island of Haiti.

6. **Are there any Prince Hall Lodges named after a President of the United States?**

John F. Kennedy No. 326, Louisa, Virginia.

7. **How many Prince Hall Grand Lodges have compiled a history?**

There are a few:

(a) *History of the Grand Lodge of Ohio* by William H. Parham and Jeremiah A. Brown.

(b) *Prince Hall Masonry in New York State* by Harry A. Williamson.

(c) *Footprints of Prince Hall Masonry in New Jersey* by Aldrage Cooper.

(d) *History of Prince Hall Grand Lodge of Ohio* by Charles H. Wesley.

(e) *History of Prince Hall Freemasonry in Kentucky* by William Henry Ballard, Sr.

(f) *The Story of the Illinois Prince Hall Grand Lodge: An Afro-American Tradition - 1952-1982* by William H. Hardy.

(g) *A History of the Most Worshipful Stringer Grand Lodge: Our Heritage is our Challenge* by Alferdteen Harrison.

8. **Are there any Prince Hall Lodges to be found outside of the Continental United States?**

(a) P.H.G.L. of Bahamas

(b) P.H.G.L. of Ontario in Canada

(c) P.H.G.L. of Alaska

(d) California has a lodge in Honolulu

(e) Washington has two lodges in Vancouver, B.C.

(f) Minnesota has a Lodge in Winnipeg, Manitoba and one in Edmonton, Alberta, Canada.

(g) New York has lodges in Guyana and Georgetown in South America, two in Barbados, one in St. Martin, N.A., and St. Lucia in the West Indies.

(h) Florida has two lodges in Belize, Central America.

9. **Are there any Research Lodges in the Prince Hall Order?**

This writer is not aware of any, but there have been a number. The first was the Prince Hall Lodge of Research of New York which received a dispensation in 1923. Its proceedings were named *Phlorony* after the first letters in each word of the title of the Lodge. New Jersey had a research lodge in 1952. Indiana also had a research lodge which later became a Chapter of the Phylaxis Society.

**10. What is the Phylaxis Society?**

An international research organization composed of Prince Hall Freemasons. It publishes a quarterly publication named *The Phylaxis*. It adopted the organizational structure of the mainstream Philalethes Society. It is well-known in Masonic circles today and many mainstream Freemasons subscribe to its publication, with a handful having been named Honorary Fellows of the Society.

**11. Are any Lodges attached to Colleges and Universities?**
There are a few:

The Jno. G. Lewis, Jr. Lodge, Southern University, in Baton Rouge, Louisiana; "Cap" Johnson Lodge at Alcorn State University; Wayne Williams Lodge at Southern University and a Lodge at Mississippi Valley State University, all three under the Jurisdiction of Stringer Grand Lodge (P.H.A.) in Mississippi.

**12. Is there a Prince Hall Masonic Collection maintained?**

Yes, at the Schomburg Center for Research and Black Culture, New York Public Library at 515 Lenox Avenue, New York City is the Harry A. Williamson collection on Prince Hall Masonry, named after the famous Masonic historian.

**13. Are any Prince Hall Lodges named after famous Black Americans?**

Yes, a few:

(a) Prince Hall - too numerous to name.

(b) Martin Luther King, Jr. No. 29, Chandler, AZ; No. 294, Spring Hope, NC, and No. 65, Renton, Washington.

(c) Booker T. Washington, No. 316, Forrest City, Arkansas named after the famous teacher, also No. 108, Hazard, KY; No. 87, Berlin Maryland; No. 78, Bridgeport, OH; and No. 274, Rock Hill, SC.

(d) George W. Carver No. 481, Cult, Arkansas; No. 95, Wyandanch, NY and No. 255, San Antonio, TX.

(e) Thomas Waller, No., 45, Los Angeles, CA, named after the musician "Fats" Waller.

(f) Daniel "Chappie" James, Jr. Military Lodge No. 27, Lowry AFB, CO. Delaware also has a Lodge named after General James.

(g) Paul L. Dunbar, No. 219, Jacksonville, FL; No. 19, Brockton, MA; No. 196, Chattanooga, TN; and No. 69, Mexia, TX.

(h) Fred Douglass Memorial No. 630, Miami, FL; No. 99, in Wichita, Kansas, and No. 72, Russellville, KY. There are a number of others but the last name is spelled differently.

(i) Oscar J. Dunn No. 85, Shreveport, La, named after the Lt. Governor and Grand Master of Louisiana.

(j) C.C. Antonie No. 185, Shreveport, LA, named after the Lt. Governor.

(k) Roscoe C. Cartwright No. 129, Upper Marlboro, MD, named after the Army General.

(l) Crispus Attucks No. 24, Ayer, MA, named after the first Black to have died for America.

(m) Peter Salem No. 40, Detroit, Michigan.

(n) Jimmie Lunceford No. 45, Detroit, Michigan.

(o) H.R. Revels No. 3, Natchez, MS., named after the first Black United States Senator

(p) Richard Allen No. 30, Philadelphia, Pennsylvania named after the founder and the Bishop of the African Methodist Episcopal Church.

(q) Absalom Jones No. 109, Easton, Pennsylvania named after the organizer of the St. Thomas Episcopal Church in Philadelphia. Jones was ordained and became the first Negro rector in the United States. He was also the first Grand Master of the Prince Hall Grand Lodge of Pennsylvania. He and Richard Allen were members of African Lodge No. 459, of Philadelphia.

14. **Can you give some reason why The Grand Lodge of England does not recognize Prince Hall Freemasonry?**

Harry A. Williamson, responding to this question, wrote: First of all it must be realized that the United Grand Lodge of England is an "aristocratic" rather than a "democratic" Masonic institution. Examine its Constitution and one will learn that certain regulations contained therein indicate clearly that it operates as a "caste system" to a great extent; the nobility plays a very high part in the English Masonic system.

The peculiar workings of English Masonry are amply illustrated in at least two known incidents within the last decade and these are:

(a) About the years 1940 and 1941, officials of the Grand Lodge of England sent appeals to mainstream American jurisdiction for financial help to assist in relieving persons who had been bombed out of their homes and lost all their belongings. Learning of such appeals, the Prince Hall Craft in New York sent a donation for that purpose in 1941. *But Mr. Sydney A. White, Grand Secretary, wrote that his Grand Lodge could not accept the donation and it was returned to the Prince Hall Brethren.*

(b) In July of 1951, a Prince Hall Mason accompanied by a member of a London lodge, visited the Temple on Great Queen Street that the former might have an opportunity to inspect the building, but after considerable hesitancy, one of the clerks informed the English member that the Prince Hall Mason could not see the interior of the Temple because he belonged to a Masonic grand jurisdiction which is not on the list of those recognized by the Grand Lodge of England.

Although the Prince Hall Fraternity is a direct descendent from the Grand Lodge of England, its refusal to recognize the Negro order may be due to the following suggested reasons:

(a) Influence and pressure brought to bear through both personal contact and correspondence with many mainstream American Masons whose race and color prejucices are deeper in their minds than are the tenets of Freemasonry. They remind one of the leopard who cannot change his spots, for, the Holy Bible upon the altars of their lodges is not strong enough to cause them to live up to their sworn obligations.

(b) The Grand Secretary has written that his Grand Lodge adheres to certain "rigid rules" when it comes to the United States but it closes its eyes to the fact that England does not recognize nor adhere to "exclusive territorial jurisdicaiton" anywhere else throughout the world; it fails to observe that rule on its own account in South Africa, Brazil, Chile, the East and West Indies. It is a poor "rigid rule" that will not work both ways.

(c) If "exclusive jurisdiction" is so rigidly adhered to, why did the Grand Lodge of England permit the Grand Lodge of Ireland to erect Leavarre Lodge No. 646, at Farnborough, Hants, in 1932? Is not Hants English territory? Consistency, thou art a jewel. And, by the way, English officials participated in the ceremonies of the erection of that Irish Lodge on English soil.

15. **Recognition has always been and continues to be a major concern and goal of Prince Hall Freemasonry. How many times has the Prince Hall Fraternity petitioned for recognition from mainstream Freemasonry?**

(a) Members of Boyer Lodge, No. 1, at New York City, petitioned the mainstream Grand Lodge of that State for recognition in 1845, but the prayer was denied at the annual session of the Grand Lodge in 1846.[1]

(b) In 1871, eight Blacks who had obtained the degrees in the Lodge of St. Andrew (mainstream) at Boston, applied to the Grand Lodge of Massachusetts for the privilege to establish a lodge for themselves in the above city and to be known under the title of "Thistle Lodge," but the same was denied.[2]

(c) In 1868, 72 members of the Prince Hall Grand Lodge of Massachusetts submitted a petition for recognition to the mainstream Grand Lodge, but the prayer was denied.[3]

(d) Upon three different occasions members of the Prince Hall Jurisdiction in the State of Michigan applied to the mainstream Grand Lodge therein and each application was denied; these petitions were as follow:

1. In 1874[4]    2. In 1899    3. In 1912[5]

(e) In 1847, a group of Blacks who were not Freemasons, applied to the Grand Lodge of Massachusetts for the degrees and the request was denied.[6]

(f) In 1869, the Grand Master, together with a group of Prince Hall Brethren, submitted a petition to the Grand Lodge in the State of Ohio for recognition and it was denied.[7]

(g) The Digest of Proceedings of the Grand Lodge of New York, 1781/1852, contains matter pertaining to the petition of Boyer Lodge, No. 1, (see No. 1 Above).[8]

(h) At the session of the Grand Lodge of Ohio held in 1875, a lodge whose membership consisted mostly of men of German birth, presented a resolution to that body proposing that if the Prince Hall body in the same state would change its title to "African Grand Lodge" and confine its work to persons of African descent, the mainstream Grand Lodge would accord it fraternal recognition.

When the matter came to a vote at the session for 1876, the resolution was lost by the slim margin of 60 out of more than 700 votes cast.[9]

## 16. Give titles to works written by Prince Hall Freemasons?

(a) *The Negro Mason in Equity* by Samuel W. Clark of Ohio.

(b) *The Origin and Objects of Ancient Freemasonry, its Introduction into the United States and Legitimacy Among Colored Men* by Martin R. Delany of Pennsylvania.

This is the very first work known to be printed on the subject from the pen of a Prince Hall Freemason. The work is exceedingly rare, but appeared in several issues of the *Phylaxis* magazine in 1976.

(c) *A History of Freemasonry Among Negroes in America* by Harry E. Davis.

(d) *Freemasonry Among American Negroes* and also *The Prince Hall Primer* by Harry A. Williamson of New York.

(e) *History of Freemasonry Among the Colored People of North America* by Wiliam H. Grimshaw of Washington,

D.C. This work has been of much concern as the author allowed his imagination to run riot.

(f) *The National Grand Lodge* by Alexander Graham Clark of Iowa.

(g) *Prince Hall and His Followers* by George W. Crawford of Connecticut.

(h) *Footprints of Prince Hall Masonry in New Jersey* by Aldrage B. Cooper of New Jersey.

(i) *History of the Grand Lodge of Ohio* by William H. Parham and Jeremiah A. Brown of Ohio.

(j) *Truth Is The Rock of Defense* by Salomon I. Bayard of New Jersey.

(k) *The Mission and Opportunity of the Negro Mason, The Significance of Brotherhood,* and *Prince Hall: Pioneer of Negro Masonry* all by John Bruce of New York.

(l) *An Appeal to the Free Masons Working Under the Jurisdiction of the "National Grand Lodge"* by A.W.A. DeLeon of California.

(m) *Sermon by Rev. John Marrant,* Chaplain of African Lodge No. 459, and delivered June 24, 1789.

(n) *Masonic Text Book* by Harrison L. Harris, M.D. of Virginia.

(o) *A Charge by Prince Hall,* June 24, 1797, at Menotomy, Massachusetts.

(p) *An Investigation of the Standing and Recognition of the National Compact York Masons* by T. Percival of South Carolina.

(q) *Centennial Oration of William L. Reed,* September 10, 1908, Boston Massachusetts.

(r) *Grand Lodge Jurisdiction Claims, or War of Races; Letters in Vindication of the National Grand Lodge of Ancient, Free and Accepted Masons of the United States of North America;* and *Caste Among Masons* all by Lewis Hayden of Massachusetts.

(s) *The History of the Prince Hall Grand Lodge of the State of Ohio 1849-1971* by Charles H. Wesley of Washington, D.C.

(t) *Prince Hall: Life and Legacy* by Charles H. Wesley.

(u) *Black Square & Compass: 200 Years of Prince Hall Freemasonry* by Joseph A. Walkes, Jr. of Leavenworth, Kansas.

(v) *History of Prince Hall Freemasonry in Kentucky* by William Henry Ballard, Sr. of Kentucky.

(w) *Great Black Men of Masonry: Qualitative Black Achievers who were Freemasons* by Joseph Mason Andrew Cox of New York.

(x) *The Story of the Illinois Prince Hall Grand Lodge: An Afro-American Tradition 1852-1982* by William H. Hardy of Illinois.

17. The controversy which has raged for over a century concerning the statutes of the Prince Hall Fraternity has produced a vast amount of literature. Few are acquainted with Bro. Willis N. Brent, the Grand Secretary of my Grand Lodge of Missouri. In his report on Foreign Correspondence in 1976, he put together a most worthy paper. While later day research has shed more light on Prince Hall, the man and Masonic leader (which of course was not available to Bro. Brent) yet, his report has much merit, and I reproduce it in full to rescue it from the pages of the past, so it may be enjoyed by our present day readers.

## REPORT
### on
### FOREIGN CORRESPONDENCE
### 1776 CENTENNIAL NUMBER 1876
### Reviewing the Course of Freemasonry Among Colored Men
### OUR GREETING
*"Watchman, What of the night?*
*The Watchman said, the morning cometh."*

That seems pertinent. These Foreign Correspondence Committees, are, "so to speak," watchmen upon the tower. Keeping sleepless vigil they are ever ready to sound the alarm. They are vigilant and note any indication of departure from the beaten path. Resting under a real or fancied security, the Craft may at least have the assurance that these "watchmen" will faithfully report, if not correctly interpret, the "signs of the times." The pleasant reception given our last Annual Report is the excuse for our reappearance. With this our term of service ends and to our collaborators we say adieu. First, we call attention to a topic of current discussion:

## COLORED MASONS AND THEIR OPPONENTS

It would seem strange that after the lapse of a century the origin and history of masonry among colored men should still be matters of doubt, and hence of discussion. We venture the statement, that in the whole range of topics in our Centennial history there is none which is more obscure, or the subject of greater misapprehension. It is a misfortune, inseparable from human conduct, that remedial measures are rarely considered with the spirit of fairness essential to a proper estimate of their real tendency to advance the common good; and that this spirit is more likely to be diminished than promoted by those occasions which, by their nature, require the utmost fairness and impartiality. An inquiry into the legitimacy of colored Freemasons is such a case. To those whose minds have been thus directed it could not appear surprising that the material facts in our history should remain so long obscured, when their disclosure was essentially dependent upon the important changes of the last decade. Changes that may be viewed in so many lights and relations, that touch the springs of so many passions and interest, and excite dispositions unfriendly to a candid and accurate judgement of the race.

We fully understand the difficulties of this discussion, arising from prejudices of opinion and from adverse conclusions, in many cases, strong and sincere as our own. We fully and painfully realize that we are in a small minority with few to whom we may look for sympathy or support.

And we are not insensible to the greatness and compactness of the organization which confronts us—as sensitive as it is powerful, possessing the power to make the whole system shake and tremble at its touch. But while these considerations may properly prompt us to caution and reserve, they cannot change the demands of justice, our convictions of duty and our determination to perform it. Grateful to the noble men who have undertaken to present our case, to the organizations which have exemplified the greatness of masonic principles by extending to us the hand of fraternal acknowledgement, we are not free from the conviction that "he who would be free must himself strike the blow."

With some, it is already too evident, from their confession, that they have scanned the proposition to reorganize colored Masons, not only with the predisposition to censure, but with a predetermination to condemn. With respect to the weight of their opinions, passing over the possible designs they may have upon us, these characters may be referred to either of two classes: the bigot, who sees no higher good than the ends of relief and profit to himself; and the vain socialist whose inclinations or endowments of mind make him careless of the principles of justice, so long as he attends to the refinements of the Institution. The former assures us that "Even if it could be shown that Negro Masons are regular and legitimate, he would take a long and last farewell of the order when they are admitted." The latter recalls the Quixotic Spaniard who said, "Take away everything else, but leave me my delusion."

While we cannot hope to win the one, nor enlighten the other, we know that men in such erroneous state of mind find a comfort in spreading the contagion of their faults. It is therefore not surprising that when they have written concerning the legitimate origin of Freemasonry among colored men in America, they would generally have shown the temper, not of judges, but of uncandid, malevolent advocates.

But they are considering, not a speculative matter, but a series of well authenticated facts, which have a direct and practical connection with the most important details in the early history of American white Masons.

Placing ourselves upon the ground of our opponents, we are staked on three chances; the regularity, permanence and proper development of the first organization, and we may add a sentiment favorably disposed to the granting what is due. Any one of these failing, we are doomed. Whatever may be the force of our method in dealing with the other questions, there is but little reason to expect a favorable judgement unless we shall first succeed in gaining the last one.

It is not generally conceded that the dawn of Freemasonry among colored men was at Boston as early as 1774. Lodge No. 243, of the Grand Lodge of Ireland, was attached to the fifty-ninth Regiment of British troops, stationed at Boston. This army lodge united with the Grand Lodge of Dr. Warren in 1774, and in it, just prior or subsequent to the union, Prince Hall and his companions were made Masons. It is immaterial to fix the exact date, further than that it occured in the year mentioned, when Dr. Warren was in full control of St. Andrews, the most prosperous Grand Lodge on the continent.

The conferring of Masonic degrees upon colored men, was an act unparalleled in its political and social significance. British Masons, in their army Lodge, practically demonstrated the sublime principles which two years later Thomas Jefferson wrote in his remarkable Declaration. With them, these were great vital principles; the mightiest factor in the history of nations. With Jefferson and his associates, these were "glittering generalities," not fully understood when announced in the holy Declaration of Independence, "they have been undergoing definition; they have been defined by convulsion and trial, individual and social experience." They have been extending through Church and State; they have been at work throughout the nation, and they have been aiming to eliminate and cast off every species of injustice and proscription in our social instructions. "We are yet quivering from the mighty throes of the desperate, but necessary struggle of political and civil purgation. These have gone out to arouse new forces and stir the nations to the ends of the earth." By the acquiescence in the act of Lodge

No. 243, Dr. Warren and his Grand Lodge practically ratified the assertion of the political and civil rights of colored men, eight years before Massachusetts had abolished the institution of slavery by a decision of its Supreme Court.

Dr. Warren acquiesced in the existence of colored Masons, or he could never have received the Irish Lodge into his Grand Lodge. And yet, its historic connection with St. Andrews is clear and indisputable. The relation of colored men to the State rendered the affiliation of Prince Hall and his associates with any of the Warren Lodges inexpedient; they understood and appreciated the rivalship between the respective Lodges of Warren and Price, and they appreciated still higher, the splendid services Warren was rendering the cause of American liberty.

The sentiments of this brilliant man and accomplished Mason leave us no room to doubt, that with respect to the colored Masons, he entertained as he did upon all questions, the most liberal and advanced views. His career was singularly brief and memorable. Leaving a successful practice, he plunged into the political arena on the passage of the "Stamp Act, " lending to the cause his trenchant pen and graceful oratory. Physician, orator, statesman, and soldier, he did honor to these several vocations. "Freedom and equality," he wrote, "is the state of nature; it is absurd to attempt to impose a cruel yoke upon a people who look upon their liberties, not merely as arbitrary grants, but as their unalienable, eternal rights." He coveted and obtained the perilous honor of pronouncing the memorial oration of Crispus Attucks, and his associates of the Boston massacre of 1770; when Adams and Quincy openly avowed that the attack led by the mulatto upon the British soldiers, was willful and unprovoked.

The secret mental history of Warren, and the steps by which he was gradually led on from his former exclusiveness to an advanced position would form the most curiously interesting phenomenon of his life. His unspairing attacks on every form and species of injustice and proscription caused him to be pushed to the front as the champion of liberalism, and apparently accepting the adventurous honor, he entered with zeal into the contest with proscription of every kind.

It seems inconceivable, therefore, that he could have been designedly instrumental in proscribing his fellow men and the conferring of Masonic degrees upon Colored men by British Masons at Boston must have met the approbation of his conscience. Whether an informal recognition can be reconciled in legal speculation, is a matter of no consequence. It is reconciled in policy and ethics ought to be adjusted, not to human's reasoning, but to human nature.

The authority from which they derived their Freemasonry, was high and reputable. The soldiers of the various European States, on their return through the remnants of the Greek empire, from the crusades under the guidance of Peter the Hermit, gathered whatever remained of literary excellence, and transported it to Europe; then the cloud of intellectual darkness began to disappear, and the flame of learning opened over the Continent amid the clash of arms and turmoil of Revolution. British soldiers brought over the embers of liberty; their own misguided conduct fanned it into a flame. And they planted in the minds of the hearts of black men the spirit and mysteries of Freemasonry.

Such are the circumstances attending the origin of Freemasonry among Colored men. Passing from their origin to their organization, we turn to well authenticated history for the facts which follow.

In 1775, African Lodge was duly founded under the same auspices which had given to Prince Hall and his associates Masonic light and received authority from the same source, which had, more than forty years previous, established St. John's Lodge at Boston. These two circumstances, distinct, and yet in their bearing closely connected, are of infinite importance. They must come again and again under consideration; for they are important, not only as showing the feelings of the two American Lodges at Boston, toward the Irish Lodge and its colored issue, but as clearly demonstrating by the course of Dr. Warren, and the action of the London Grand Lodge, that "Jurisdictional claims" were not then regarded as of special importance. The experiment seems to have been eminently satisfactory, and during nine years, the attitude of the white toward the colored Masons, was pacific; and in 1784, a charter was granted to the colored Masons by the Grand Lodge of England, constituting "African Lodge No. 459." There is no recored or tradition that either of the two Lodges at Boston demurred to this action.

Dr. Mackey entertains some notions on this point, which, if they were generally accepted, could not fail of completing our ruin. After paying his compliments to "the Grand Lodge of Ohio, and the colored Masons," he says:

*"In 1784, the Grand Lodge of England granted a charter to Prince Hall and other colored men, for holding a lodge in Boston. As there was already a Grand Lodge of Massachusetts, it is evident that the granting of the charter was illegal, and that, according to the recognized principles of American Masonic law, the said charter was null and void."*

He is so eager to attack our legitimacy, that he provides but indifferently for his own defense. Where would this reasoning land him? If priority of claim gave the right of jurisdiction, then St. John's Lodge possessed it; and the granting of the charter to Dr. Warren for St. Andrews, "was illegal," and the "said charter, according to the recognized principles of American Masonic law was null and void." Eliminate from the elements which formed the union of 1792, that known as St. Andrews, and where does it place the Grand Lodge of Massachusetts, and its descendants?

There are opposite and conflicting opinions of American Masons, respecting the reputation of St. Andrews, or Massachusetts Grand Lodge, which our learned and zealous opponent would do well to remove, ere he directs her monitory finger toward us. We propose to impeach her by the voice of one of her own associates. A Committee of

Foreign Correspondence of the Grand Lodge of New Hampshire, after an exhaustive examination into the early history of the Grand Lodge of the commonwealth of Massachusetts, made the following remarkable report as the result of their conclusions. They say:

*"In Masachusetts there was no legal Grand Lodge till the union of 1792. The American doctrine of Grand Lodge Jurisdiction has grown up since; the establishment of the African Lodge at Boston, by authority of a charter from the Grand Lodge of England, and not elsewhere, fully received even now, besides there was then no Grand Lodge of Massachusetts, or in that State, whose rights could be interfered with; for notwithstanding the claim to antiquity of that Grand Lodge, it was not formed till 1792, and the two Provincial Grand Lodges, before existing in that colony, both expired in 1775, by the death of their Provincial Grand Masters. The Massachusetts Grand Lodges did not pretend to meet after the death of Warren, and although St. John's Grand Lodge did have some sort of meeting, probably no law that has ever existed in Masonry anywhere would hold such meetings regular."* (N.H.J.C. 1870)

Such is the recent judgement of Masonic investigations. This postition Mr. Gardner attempted to assail in an elaborate address before the Grand Lodge of Massachusetts, March 7th, 1870, and his agruments have furnished the data for all subsequent opponents.

Contemporaneous history, in fact the recorded utterance of the St. Andrew's. To meet the charge of illegality, made by the members of St John's, a select committee was appointed to examine into their condition and report. Their conclusion was:

1. *"That the commission from the Grand Lodge of Scotland, granted to our late Grand master, Joseph Warren, Esq., having died with him, of course his deputy, whose appointment was derived from his nomination, being no longer in existence, we see ourselves without a head and without a single Grand Officer; and of consequence it is evident, that*

*not only the Grand Lodge, but all the particular Lodges under its jurisdiction, must cease to assemble, the brethren dispersed, and Ancient Masonry be extinct in this part of the world."*

2. *"That in consequence of a summons from the former Grand officers to the Master and Wardens of all the regular constituted Lodges, a Grand communication was held to consult and advise on some means to preserve the intercourse of the brethren."*

3. *"That the political head of this country having destroyed this connection and correspondence between the subjects of these States and the country from which the Grand Lodge originally derived its commissioned authority, and the principles to the comands of the civil authority of the country they reside in, the brethren did assume an elective supremacy; and under it chose a Grand Master and Grand Officers, and erected a Grand Lodge with independent powers and prerogatives, to be exercised, however, on principles consistent with, and subordinate to, the regulations pointed out in the Constitutions of Ancient Masonry."* (Masonry in Massachusetts, J.W.S. Mitchell, *Masonic Signet*, Vol. VII, 1852.)

This has been a rich theme of declamation, and the only refuge left, for those who condemn colored Masons upon the ground of the precedent rights of the St. Andrews Lodges, is the visionary supposition that, that committee was misguided by some inconsiderate leaders like the Grand Master of Ohio and his committee.

The doctor has a flight of fancy; he sees a "fire-brand," and incipient "conflagration," and like another Aeneas, he resolves to defend his native Troy, and with his fidus Achates he will quit it only for the devouring flames.

These reasonings of a writer whose talents have had no inconsiderable share of applause of American Masons, does not seem otherwise than an attmept to experiment upon their discernment. The facts which disprove his proposition are no longer objects of speculation. The records of the Grand

Lodge of Massachusetts disprove him. Whatever may have been their ambition, it is incontestibly true that in 1784 St. John's and St. Andrews exercised with African Lodge concurrent jurisdiction at Boston. If we accept the dubious account of Robert Macoy that the Massachusetts Grand Lodge was formed in 1769 by St. Andrews, in conjunction with three British Army Lodges, we are still in a dilemma where to place St. John's Lodge. But there are grave historical doubts respecting this account, and we prefer to go back to those plain statements which are more obviously in accordance with accepted facts.

Findel, in his elaborate history of Freemasonry, recounting its early history in America, informs us:

*"At a meeting of the Brethren at the festival of St. John the Evangelist, 1769, Bro. Joseph Warren received from the Earl of Dalhouise, then Grand Master of Scotland, a warrant nominating the said brother Provincial Grand Master of the so-styled Ancient Masons in Boston, within a circuit of a hundred miles, with which office he was formally invested at the same meeting."*

This lucid statement clears up for us any doubts that remained respecting the status of St. Andrews in 1769. The appointment of General Warren by the Grand Master of Scotland, his acceptance of that trust, and the ratification of these several acts by the members assembled, were each and all admissions fixed for us the limit and signification of the word *Provincial*.

*"The appointment of a Provincial Grand Master for large district, is a prerogative of the Grand Master, by whom, or in his absence, by his deputy, a patent may be granted, during pleasure, to such brother of eminence and ability in the Craft as may be thought worthy of the appointment. By this patent he is invested with a rank and power, in his particular district, similar to those possessed by the Grand Master himself."*

It seems evident, then, that at the time under review, there was no Grand Lodge of Massachusetts, and that Boston was a district under the putative jurisdiction of Scotland, and Warren a deptuy under the Earl of Dalhousie. In 1773, by a similar document, his jurisdiction was extended over the whole continent of America. Henry Price held a similar but precedent appointment, and exercised similar authority from the Grand Lodge of England. While Freemasonry was thus spreading throughout every part of the country, the two organizations in Boston which, from the circumstance of their rapid increase and prosperity, were called Grand Lodges, were working under different systems, showing mutual hostility, until 1775, the War of Independence came, harmonizing by its common dangers and demands all the differences and dissensions, and suspending at the same time all signs of activity.

The death of General Warren had a palsying effect upon the members of St. Andrews. On the 8th of March, 1777, the lodges under the jurisdiction of the late Deputy Grand Master held a meeting to consider the condition of their late organization, and to devise means to resuscitate or reorganize it. It was the general opinion that this commission was a personal emolument and that their tenure, being dependent upon him, became extinct with his death. Whether this reasoning was correct, or was intended to pave the way for a subsequent course of action is not for us to determine, but it was the basis of their action, and fully establishes our proposition: that they had never regarded their organization as anything but subordinate to the Grand Lodge of Scotland. Here we demure to the opinion of Dr. Mackey. The progress of African Lodge from 1775 to 1777 was satisfactory, and fully equal to that of St. John's and St. Andrews during the first two years of their existence, and the action of the members of the extinct Warren organization no more affected the status of African Lodge than the St. John's Lodge.

After due consideration they determined to form *de novo* a Grand Lodge, and in due course elected and installed Joseph Webb Grand Master. The right to form an independent

Grand Lodge may be justly conceded, but it is concluded that such an admission destroys the claims of the other organizations existing at the same time and wholly independent of its power and authority. And now, on the very threshold, we encounter this objection as a final settlement, in principle and substance, of the question of Regularity, and that all discussion of it is closed. Both the Grand Lodges by consolidation in 1792 united in this declaration, and their descendants throughout the length and breadth of the Republic have joined in its promulgation. To this combined effort we have made but feeble reply, for, with flagrant inconsistency, it forbids the very discussion, which it pretends to challenge. From a notorious innovation imposed upon a powerless minority at one period, it should be understood that the rights and privileges accorded to American Freemasons be applied equally among all men.

But no unanimity of Masonic journalists can long uphold the groundless assumption, that a declaration, or series of declarations, under the name of *Masonic Law*, or however called, is final, when made in violation of constitutional guarantees, the landmarks and the inherent rights of Masons. There is no position which rests on clearer principles, than that no act, except his own, can destroy the inherent rights of a Mason. No legislative act, or device contrary to this fundamental truth can be valid. And every act of original or delegated authority contrary to the tenor of this general principle, is void. The joining of the two Grand Lodges, and the startling announcement of the claim of exclusive territorial jurisdiction may have been based upon the principle deduced from the precedent of 1717—but the contrary conditions did not warrant their sweeping proscription.

The Grand Lodge of London had made a similar announcement, but under widely different circumstances. The mission of that organization was a high and honored one. The small remnant of Operative Masons and their associates dispersed, and, disheartened by a train of unfavorable circumstances, dragged on a miserable existence at the opening of the eighteenth century. Gathering in the remnants of an Institution which had gone to pieces amid the general wreck and decay of the Middle Ages, Operative Masons revived and restored, improved and promoted it, when in England and Europe there scarce remained the shadow of an organization. To lay a foundation as broad as its benevolence, and as deep as its morality, to rebuild, remodel, reconstruct, these were the aims in the establishment of Modern Freemasonry. However much we may condemn in the removal of certain sources of strength, the cutting away of certain ancient privileges, the modifying of distinct and essential principles, the radical changes in its form and construction, it must still be acknowledged that the plan for restructuring and rebuilding Freemasonry has been grandly executed.

Findel bitterly complains of this new design of Freemasonry at the close of his examination of the "First Period" of the history of Freemasonry. "When trying to present to our view," he says, "a general idea of the cause of the development of Freemasonry from 1717 to 1783, our eyes can only rest with complete satisfaction upon the first thirty years of its existence, the happy period when it was in its infancy, and a glorious epoch when Freemasonry was first founded, cultivated, propagated, the time when inward peace and unity prevailed. Being more universal in its tendencies than other confederations, embracing all mankind, and aiming at promoting their moral, spiritual and physical advancement, it ought to have, from the very beginning, insisted upon the recognition of the inviolability of the general laws of the Order; upon complete unity on essential points, and upon maintaining the dignity of the institution in all its purity, though in everything else leaving its members perfect freedom and independence.

"The Mother Lodge of England had, on the one hand, been guilty of great neglect, and had previously sinned, while on the other hand many events had combined to retard its progress. The Grand Lodges of Ireland and Scotland were formed without the co-operation and participation of England, and without a friendly understanding existing between them; and this was not a favorable omen for their laboring together in one common cause for their unity of spirit, nor for the healthy development of the Fraternity. Nor had the society long existed before a deplorable schism broke out in the Brotherhood for a second Grand Lodge was formed in England by the schismatic 'Ancient Masons,' and thus a severing element sprung up in the very heart of this 'union of unions.' ...Lodges and Grand Lodges arose and vanished; systems appeared and disappeared, connections were made and broken; the Grand Lodge of England, who herself formed her own constitutions on hierarchical principles, and this in many respects deteriorated from its worth, designed to recognize connections with, and allied herself to Grand Lodges which stood on quite another foundation from what she did, with other aims and purposes, and unable to adduce any proof of the lawfulness of their origin. In a word, the record is one of obscurity, ignorance and confusion, sometimes even of delusion and manifest fraud."

This description is equally as applicable to the first period of American Masonic history as to the events in the early history of European Masonry. There arose the same deplorable schism, different systems appeared, everywhere causing confusion and discord, and ceaseless yearnings for revenge. Grand Lodges came into being with other aims and purposes, with records of obscurity, confusion and manifest fraud. The Grand Lodge of Massachusetts (St. Andrew's,) whose very existence itself, in the language of Dr. Mackey, is a standing protest against "the recognized principles of American Masonic law," by formal announcement declared the St. John Masons irregular, and for a purpose which may have been neither just nor honorable, subsequently contracted an alliance with them. In this arrangement the African Lodge was entirely unprovided for; and we owe it to the prevailing sentiment of the times to say that the omission was wholly intentional.

The policy was unjust and arbitrary, pursuing a method of procedure without precedent. Force constituted at once its principle and its law. In all contests between the members of African and their white brethren in every time and place, the authority of justice and law has been discarded; difference of condition is considered as a crime; suspicion is condemnation; nonconformity, Masonic death. Policy knows no law but force in its dealings with the weak, and rejects the authority of time and the lessons of its own experience.

If it could be shown, from considerations of necessity or convenience, that the claim of exclusive territorial jurisdiction was conceded by St. John and the African Lodge, and that *in fact* they exercised it without opposition, still in contemplation of law, the presumption would be stongly against them. It is a maxim of common law that there is no right without a remedy, nor any legal authority without a legal course to carry it into effect.

Let the authority in question be tried by the rule. St. Andrew's, like its contemporaries, was established by foreign grant admissibly equal in point of credit. Its growth and success was disproportional to the others, but it would require an immense stretch of the imaginaiton to conclude from this fact that the rights of the others were swallowed up. If mere superiority or difference of circumstances were to exercise an arbitrary power in directing the conduct of the strong toward the weak, the mutual intercourse of mankind would be nothing more than a contention between positive and equitable right.

Society would be a state of controversy, and the law itself would be injustice. On this general ground we conclude that the mere assumption of exclusive jurisdiction would be insufficient to detract anything from our inherent rights.

And, as respects their legitimacy, regularity and legality, St. John's, St. Andrew's and African Lodges went down to the War of Independence equal before Masonic law.

We are met with the objection that "African Lodge 459, as it was called, was never recognized by the Grand Lodge of

Massachusetts." All but the force of the objection is admitted. Prince Hall and his members were witnesses of the fierce denunciations heaped upon the St. John's Masons, and they naturally concluded that a body whose utmost energies were impotent to harm a foe, would be as powerless to aid a friend.

Dr. Mackey thus continues his brief history of the origin of "Colored Masonry":

*"After some time, it ceased its connection with the Grand Lodge of England, and about the beginning of the present century, its registration (African Lodge) was stricken from the rolls of that Grand Lodge, by which act its Masonic life was as effectually destroyed as would be a man's life by the cutting off of his head."*

We do not believe that the fact which he states has ever been seriously denied, but it certainly would require an appeal to the imagination to draw from thence the conclusion that its Masonic life was thereby destroyed. We suppose it is recorded in the books that a youth must of necessity die because the ordinary occurrences of life happen to separate him from his mother.

The reason for the action attributed to the Grand Lodge of England, so far as it implies a censure of black Masons, is entirely unfounded, and as it affects their regularity, has no more significance than a similar action in striking from its register the grants to the St. John Lodges in Boston at the time of the union of 1813. Intercourse between the Grand Lodge of England and African Lodge was cordial and uninterrupted until the proclamation of the president, Mr. Madison, in 1810, prohibited all intercourse with Great Britain.

The events of the War of 1812 are not entirely forgotten. The impressment of American sailors, the capture of American vessels and annihilation of American commerce, and the national character trampled under foot by an arrogant foe, were wrongs sufficient to kindle patriotic zeal. Congress was called together early in November and, on the

recommendation of the President, they made active prepara-
tions for war. It was hoped that Great Britain, seeing that
America was in earnest, would be willing to increase the
number of her enemies and would recede from her imperious
and aggressive position. The hope was fallacious; the English
ministry was obstinate, their majority in parliament was
subservient, and the spirit of the nation uncontrollable. So
intense and universal was the resentment of the American
people, that every man who dared to speak in favor of the
"British Orders in Council," or to palliate the outrages which
had followed their promulgation, whatever his abilities and
virtues, however isolated and obscure, whatever his condition, influence and connections, was hunted down and load-
ed with contempt and ignominy. Such was the feeling which
possessed the American people, from the declaration of war
in April, 1812, to the treaty of peace in December, 1814.

Black Masons were loyal to the government; locking up
their Masonry in faithful breasts they dedicated all to their
country, their homes, and their God. Thenceforth, there was
a practical divorcement of the guardian and ward, but the
latter had emerged from a state of dependence and, like
Joseph Webb and his associates of 1777, were prepared to
assume the direction of their own affairs. We have already
cited the ground of their declaration, (No. 3). If the reasons
were good and sufficent in the case of Webb, Revere & Co.
who, by their own admissions, were *hors de la loi*, the prin-
cipal, would certainly sustain the action of Prince Hall and
his associates. The erasure could not have been the penalty
for any misdemeanor or ommision, for there was never at
any time an arraignment; and we here cite a constitutional
provision of the Grand Lodge of England which, incorporated into our own jurisdiction, is ample authority on this
point. It recites:

ARTICLE 15. *"No Lodge shall be erased, nor any
brother expelled until the Master and Officers of the Lodge,
or the offending brother, shall have been summoned to show
cause, in the Grand Lodge, why such sentence should not be
recorded and enforced."*

Our objectors must show by the records of the said Grand Lodge that such summons was duly issued, the arraignment or default, and the subject matter of judgment entered against us. Failing in this, they stand convicted as malicious traducers. Turning from reason and the record, we introduce the evidence of a living witness—the present Grand Secretary of the Grand Lodge of England. His written statement is: That on the principle that change in the government of the country had impaired its former Masonic authority, *"he had no doubt that all the American Lodges were erased from the English register at the time when the African Lodge was erased in 1813."*

The italics are his words.

Rarely has such deception been attempted. Stripped of the glamour with which the Oracle had surrounded it, the motive appears in all its guilt and hideousness. It must be exhibited as it is, alike in its influence and its animating character, its concealed as well as manifest nature. There is an excess of refinement in the idea of having two sets of principles by which to judge one class of men, part of whom have the accident of color. Here we might leave this far-fetched imputation of neglect or misdemeanor. But the case is weaker yet. Evidence accumulates of such aptness and importance that we cannot forbear the use of it. There is another view of the question, in perfect harmony with all the proofs offered, supported by the contemporaneous history of the Grand Lodges of Europe. If the policy of African Lodge was not fully approved, our position could still be maintained. Precedents were not wanting to fully justify their course. The application of these will be readily apparent if we do not disregard well established principles. We turn for authentic testimony to the elaborate work of J.G. Findel, second edition, 1869—then whom there is no higher authority. Referring to a difference on a governmental question between the Grand Lodge of England and the Lodge of Antiquity, (No. 1,) he says:

*"The Lodge of Antiquity, which for more than sixty years had participated in the deliberations of the Grand Lodge,*

*and one of the four ancient Lodges, had renounced all claim to former principles, suddenly appealed to these immemorial privileges, setting them in opposition to the supposed uncontrollable authority of the Grand Lodge."* (P.181)

Resuming the authority it had voluntarily conceded, it continued in this attitude of opposition for thirteen years. Whether the original question at issue was conceded by the Grand Lodge, does not appear, but the right to exist separate and independent, even in oppositon to the will of the Grand Lodge, was in principle fully admitted. There may have been special reasons for its action in this case; but from the fact that a so conservative and exacting body did not take measure to coerce the fractious Lodge into submission, we must infer, that the Grand Lodge could find no warrant for so doing.

Turning to a more conservative body, Findel further informs us:

*"In Scotland, as well as England, a sort of Masonic supreme power was formed independent of the Grand Lodge, by the Mother Lodge, Kilwinning... In 1743, the Lodge of Kilwinning receded from the Grand Lodge in consequence of its having been placed second on the roll of Lodges, and it held an independent positon until October 1807, when a reunion was effected by a Committee of both Lodges. The Mother Lodge, Kilwinning, renounced all right of granting charters, and came into the bosom of the Grand Lodge of Scotland, together with all her daughter Lodges, she being placed at the head of the roll of the Grand Lodge."* (P.416)

We think sixty-four years of undisputed independence, and the full enjoyment of the Sovereign privilege of sending her charters to every part of the globe, must have been indeed a fair test of sovereignty. Widow Kilwinning gained her suit; was prolific during her divorcement and, as one of her children turned up on this side of the water, we shall have occasion to refer to her again.

We quote further what Findel says as showing the *status* of a Lodge during its compulsory separation from the warranting power, its relation to the political authority, and ability to regulate its own course of action. On these points he observes:

"*While the French held sway in Germany, the English provincial Grand Lodge and the Lodge 'Frederich Zum weissen Pferde' suspended operations in Hanover... When the land was in the hands of the Prussians in 1806, the Lodge 'Zum Schwarzen Bar,' joined the Grand National Mother Lodge in Berlin, but only for a time, that by obeying the Prussian edict, the works might be allowed to continue with all their brilliant success,... This they were most liberally allowed to do. In 1809, their connection was again broken off.*" (P.512.)

And further, on the same points he observes:

"*When Hanover was incorporated with the Kingdom of Westphalia, and intercourse with England was rendered a difficult matter, the Provincial Lodge joined the Grand Lodge of Hamburg.*"...(P.513)

We may be permitted to make one more citation, covering not only the ground we have under review, but embodying the right of jurisdiction *in pleno*, which we have already commented upon in another place. The case is so just and applicable to the circumstances of our own, and it comes to us so well authenticated, that as to our legality and regularity, we may build our argument upon it. Narrating first the circumstances out of which grew the issue, he observes:

"*The Lodge 'Zur auf gehendin Morgenrothe' in Frankfurt O.M. was, in consequence of political events in 1814, necessitated to separate herself from the Grand Orient of France, but immediately received a warrant from the Landgrave, Carl of Hesse, at the same time as did the Lodge of Mayence. But as the Landgrave required that the Chairman and orator should be Christians, and the Jewish members opposed this determination, the Christians left the Lodge and formed a new one, which received from the Landgrave, a warrant. The Lodge 'Zur auf gehenden Morgenrothe' by the defection of her Christian brethren was shaken to her very foundation and, being opposed on all sides, demanded a Constitution from the Grand Lodge of England, which was granted without hesitation.*

*"The English Provincial Lodge of Frankfurt, appealed to the treaty concluded with London, by vitrue of which Lodges in her jurisdiction could only be erected by her, and with her consent, and she therefore protested against the conduct of the Mother Lodge. The latter however, remained firm to her purpose, most probably persuaded that it was unfriendly and unsociable to turn her back upon regularly constituted and faithful brethren, without investing them with the power to continue their work. And this right she had derived from Masonic fundamental law, as well as from the turn affairs had taken; for if the infraction of the treaty had been committed, it was certainly the act of the Provincial Lodge, who, without previously consulting the Mother Lodge, had adopted certain modifications not prescribed by law. The dispute with England, led to fruitless negotiations which lasted for years, and at length to a declaration of independence on the part of the Frankfurt Provincial Lodge, which, since 1823, was worked as the Grand Lodge of the Eclectic Union of Freemasons." (P. 514.)*

Thus, much of the evidence from the contemporary history of European Masons; and the true principles of the institution are in perfect harmony with the conclusions of history. In the light of this evidence, and the well established principles which underlie the institution, we are warranted in affirming that no act or acts of ours can be regarded as an encroachment upon its landmarks, power or constitutional limitations.

## Early Growth of Prince Hall Masonry

We now come to consider the circumstances connected with the growth of this organization.

It is to Lewis Hayden, P.G.M. of Massachusetts, that we are indebted for many of the important details connected with the early history of Freemasonry among black men. He merits the approbation of his brethren everywhere for the great assistance he has rendered in collecting, narrating and reporting the facts in connection with our early annuals; by his zeal and great industry, he stands conspicuously the first among black Masonic authors. It is his opinion that Prince Hall was commissioned, and exercised the power and authority of Deputy Grand Master, and that he was·so regarded by his contemporaries. In confirmation of this opinion, he prints in his argument on "*Grand Lodge Jurisdictional Claim,*" 1868, a communication from Colored Masons in Philadelphia, March 2nd, 1797, asking Prince Hall for authority to establish a Lodge among them. He is addressed as "Rt. W. Sir:" He is formally congratulated upon his investiture with the high and holy trust conferred by the Grand Lodge of England, and "in the name of most holy Trinity, Father, Son, and Holy Ghost, he is most respectfully solicited to grant a dispensation for an African Lodge."

The names of eleven Masons are mentioned in the application, five of whom are Master Masons. Their Masonic origins are given in detail, from which it appears that one was made in an Irish Army Lodge; four called themselves *Ancient York Masons*, and six were made in London. The genuineness of their work had been thoroughly tested by five Royal Arch Masons. They had regularly applied to the Grand Lodge of Pennsylvania for establishment and had been refused under the plea that black men living in Virginia would get to be Masons too.

This letter, which is of the utmost value, may be found, we think, in the archives of the Prince Hall Grand Lodge of Pennsylvania. It sheds a ray of light upon the whole course of Prince Hall. We have somewhere seen it stated that the same number of colored men in Pennsylvania had applied to the Grand Lodge of England for the proper authority to open a lodge, and had been referred to Prince Hall for that purpose. The internal and external evidence of the letter seems to indicate that of the number there were several well informed. The fact that six were made Masons in London would establish that point. And Peter Mantone, who was probably the author of the letter, as well as acting Master, was in possession of all the higher degrees. This granted, we think, they fully understood what authority was *competent* to grant their request. Their first application was to the Grand Lodge of Pennsylvania, which had not long before closed *sine die,* and reorganized as an independent Grand Lodge. That application was refused. Then, probably application was made to the source of all Masonic authority, the Grand Lodge of England, with the information that Prince Hall had been commissioned to represent the interests of colored Masons in America. If there is any significance to be attached to the language of the Communication from the Pennsylvania brethren, which is singularly clear and explicit, that inference is easily made. We copy its opening:

*"We congratulate you for having been invested with the high and holy trust conferred upon you by the authorities in England."*

This, we take it, is a *personal* congratulation, referring to a private honor and to duties developing solely upon Prince Hall. The information respecting it, must have come directly from the source which gave it, and we do not know why the assumption is not to be accepted, that he held a commission to constitute colored Lodges. Then follows the concluding part of the sentence:

*"Together with your success in obtaining the warrant constituting African Lodge 459."*

This is a distinct proposition, congratulating Hall for an action performed in an official capacity. As Deputy Grand Master, they congratulate him. As an officer of African Lodge, they congratulate him. If possibly, black men erred in the use of the language, how shall we explain the statement of Dr. Belknap, in the collection of the Massachusetts Historical Society? He replies:

*"Having once and again mentioned this person, I must inform you that he is Grand Master of the Lodge of Freemasons, composed wholly of blacks, and distinguished by the name of the African Lodge."*

And here we end this branch of our inquiry. While reflecting upon the difficulties of our situation, we are ready to say with Colton:

"The greatest friend of Truth is Time; her greatest enemy is Prejudice; and her constant companion is Humility."

The dispensation to Peter Montone and his associates was granted, and a similar Lodge was constituted in Rhode Island.

It is not alone by the rapid increase of lodges, that the progress of the black Masons is to be estimated; there were contrary and perplexing conditions. Masonry could be planted and flourish only upon soil favorable to liberty and equality of rights. In such reverential regard was the institution held by them, that the management of its affairs was more distinguished by prudence than zeal. So far was this feeling carried, that, when granted a dispensation to some worthy brethren to open a new Lodge, Prince Hall most positively enjoined that "no new members should be received until their warrant was obtained."

In a survey of our Masonic progress, beset with recent difficulties, our interest demands that we first get back to the old bearings. There has been a wide departure from the landmarks. The broad line of demarcation between the opinions of today and those which a century ago prevailed, can nowhere be more distinctly traced than precisely at this point. And the principles which underlie the tests applied to black Masons, have been borrowed from American laws, and are due to the exigencies of American politics. This draft of Masonic sentiment towards the creation of an ideal standard presents not only novel and intricate problems, but renders it more difficult for black Masons whose history has never been written, and whose claims are still in abeyance, to satisfy these excessive demands. From the ideal, we appeal to the real standard. From a supposed custom to the actual practice. What is the model for the organization and propagation of Freemasonry? This question will be asked and discussed with all the earnestness its importance demands. Let us hear Dr. Mackey on the subject:

*"...It is essential that not less than three Lodges shall unite in forming a Grand Lodge. Dermott, without any other authority that I can discover than his own ipse dixit, says that no less than five Lodges must concur in the formation of a Grand Lodge, and Dr. Dalcho, who was originally an Ancient York Mason, repeats the doctrine; but if this be the true state of the law, then the Grand Lodge of England, which was organized in 1717, with the concurrence of only four Lodges, must have been irregular. The fact is, there is no ancient regulation on the subject; but the necessity of three Lodges concurring is denied, from the well known principle of the civil law, that a college or corporate body must consist of three persons at least."*

Here we have the pith of the question. Different authorities of different degrees of credibility, set up different standards of excellence. Dermott the apostate, and Dr. Dalcho of the Scotch Rite, would require the concurrence of five Lodges. The Grand Lodge of England is reported to have had four. Dr. Mackey, invokes the high authority of the Roman Civil Law, and would have three. The common law of Masonry, requires but one. These several positions it is our purpose to examine. We do not suppose that any unusual weight is to be attached to the statement of Dr. Dalcho, for he is principally conspicuous for having vibrated between the York and Scotch Rites. The name of Laurance Dermott, like that of Peter, is the synonym for apostasy. His alterations of the Ancient Constitutions to make them accord with the circumstances of his spurious Grand Lodge, and his fraud in publishing the *Ahiman Rezon* as collection of genuine ancient law, do not inspire in us a high degree of confidence. Five Lodges were necessary with him, because he wished to discredit the Grand Lodge of England, and his work has been characterized as little more than a violent polemic treatise upon the regularity of that organization.

By his book, which was authority in many states during the war, all Lodges and assemblies of Masons, were held to be irregular and clandestine whose members were in favor of American independence.

The reorganization of 1717, was not effected by four Lodges, but by a mass meeting, composed of members of the four London Lodges. The preliminary meeting was composed of leading Masons, who were conspicuous for their learning, attainments, and high social position. They held a formal consultation. A committee composed of these same men prepared a plan which was adopted, not in convention, but at different periods, at the respective meetings of the four Lodges.

In February, 1717, another meeting was held, not of Lodges, but of old members, old, we presume, in contradistinction to Apprentices and Fellows for, in general, they enjoyed the privilege of participating in the transaction of business. The democratic system then prevailed. Disregarding, or not understanding the forms of the representative system, they voted the oldest Master Mason then present, into the chair, and constituted themselves a Grand Lodge *pro tempore*. On St. John the Baptist's day, June 24, the brethren again met. It is presumed, from the fact that the meeting was held on the day of the annual festival, that all members were present: Masters, Fellows and Apprentices. At this general meeting of the Craft, a Grand Master was elected by a majority of hands. All essential limitations for the government of Lodges and members were embodied in the Constitutions of 1721 and 1723. If such a method had been followed as the one in question, its importance, and especially its departure from the time honored form, would have demanded its incorporation in the body of the law. Its absence is certainly significant. The Grand Lodge of York was reviewed with *eleven* brethren, assisted by some visitors, and up to that time had remained an isolated Lodge, never having been granted a warrant of constitution. Candidates were proposed, initiation, and passing took place in the same course. (See Findel's *History on Freemasonry*, second edition, p. 166.)

Between the Grand Lodge of York and the London Grand Lodge, a fraternal correspondence was maintained, and this fact seems favorable to the opinion that their mode of procedure was not different from the established practices of the London Masons.

The Grand National Mother Lodge of the "Three Globes" at Berlin, established by Baron Bielfeld in 1740, was raised to the dignity of a Grand Lodge by Frederick the Great, King of Prussia.

The Grand Lodge Royal York of Friendship, which was formerly subordinate to the "Three Globes," under the title of the lodge *de l' Amitie*, separated from the Mother Lodge after the initiation of the Duke of York in 1765, and assumed its present position and title.

Mother Lodge, Kilwinning, of the Grand Lodge of Scotland, exercised the powers of a Grand Lodge issuing, among others, two charters for Lodges in Virginia. When a reunion was effected, it was expressly provided that her daughter Lodges should be regarded as legal. This provision was accordingly made by the Grand Lodge of Scotland.

Eleven Masons were present in the formation of the Grand Lodge of Massachusetts in 1777 all of them officers of the defunct Warren Grand Lodge, save two, and none of them in a representative capacity.

The Grand Lodge of Rhode Island, which we think is recognized by the American Grand Lodges, seems not to have conformed to the three Lodge theory.

An American author informs us that:

*"Notwithstanding the irregularity of the formation of the Grand Lodge by only two subordinates, Freemasonry has always occupied a respectable position in Rhode Island, and her membership has been composed of its best and most honored citizens."*—(Robt. Macoy, *Gen. Hist. Cyclopedia and Dictionary of Freemasonry, 1870.)*

We come now to the three Lodge theory, with which the opponents of black Masons hope to crush them. We cannot conceive what practical connection can be established between Freemasonry and the Roman Civil Law; nor why the common law of the one, should be discarded for the barbarism of the other. All this is but an attempt to transplant to the present age, institutions of the past, which comes to us already smitten with decay.

If we resort to a criterion based on the ordinances or principles on which entirely different institututions have engrafted upon Masonry, we violate principles which are antagonistic to Masonry's spirit and genius. Let us examine more closely.

We quote from high authority:

*"College, (Lat. Collegium, an association), in its primary and most general meaning, the union of several persons, (collegal, colleagues), with like powers, privileges, and customs in one office for a common end. Thus in Roman antiquity, colleges consisted of at least three persons, forming a corporation for religious, political or industrial pruposes." (The American Cyclopaedia, 1874, Vol. V. p. 56.)*

Are we to contract an unnatural alliance with religious orders by adopting the most repulsive principles upon which they were formed? Consider the pernicious influence and designs of the Jesuits upon the Institution in 1783.

Are we to connect Masonry with political bodies?

Let the rich experiences of France and Germany, and especially Spain, furnish a few lessons. Why attempt to associate what, in the very nature of things, can never be united? Can it be that this grand old institution which has come down to us with its ameliorating influences, that has seen governments flourish and decay, that has passed through a hundred revolutions unscathed, is now to terminate in that form of society in which are the elements of disorder? A society marked out with compass and rule, in which the corporation arrogates to itself everything, and the individual is to be nothing; in which the corporation is to absorb all force, all life, and in which the only end assigned to man, is personal relief.

Governments, are not an end to themselves, but a means for achieving an end, which is higher, broader, more enduring. They exist for man, not man for them. The method by which he seeks to realize social aims, is by change of form, as one after another fails of its purpose, until he finds one adapted to his condition. We need not traverse the whole extent of the Civil Law to find an enduring, vigorous principle of Government. We may turn to Masonry where we see it living, active, triumphant; where throughout revolutions and religious and political upheavals, it has been able to establish and maintain to the present, a grand and durable structure to claim our admiration, in England, Germany, and even America. In the Constitutions and Common Law, we shall look in vain for any theory or proof of the legitimacy of Prince Hall Masonry. Not only has it gained no acknowledgement in Masonic law, but in the discussion and management of its affairs, it has not even reached the dignity of exciting inquiry.

The sum of what has been here advanced is that the charge against black Masons of non-compliance with the common law, has no foundation to rest upon; that if they had not complied, they were not only warranted, but required by the circumstances in which they were placed, to exercise the independence which they assumed. How far they did comply with the requirements of the unwritten law, we propose now to consider.

African Lodge, under the direction of Prince Hall, was an eminent success. To him must be ascribed the credit of the first organization, and the procurement of its charter; to his efforts the extension growth management and subsequent reorganization. He is inseparably connected with the history of black Masons and, as the founder and propagator, sustains to them the same relation as did Price and Warren to the white. Although Hall had only the simplest rudiments of education, he possessed a remarkable talent for the adminstration of affairs united to a clear, strong judgment. And since we have referred to his want of literary culture, it would be unjust not to commend the judicious encouragement which, as a representative citizen, he gave to education and mental improvement. With a rare good sense, he thus admonishes his associates:

*"Let us lay by our recreations and all superfluities, so that we may have the means to educate our rising generation which we were wont to spend in those follies. Make you this beginning, and who knows but God may raise up some friends, or body of friends, as he did in Philadelphia, to open a school for the blacks here, as that friendly city has done there."*

Prince Hall clearly discerned, what was not so obvious to his contemporaries, that education must be the stepping stone, not only for the new organization, but also for the race. In every question that could arise between the races, he knew the immense advantage of greater talents, and superior adroitness; and the almost absolute certainty that these advantages would sustain any claim it might be convenient for their opponents to make against them.

American law, in spite of the ameliorations which grew out of independence, was neither trusty nor equitable. A system in course of development; in some points it was fashioned to suit the popular feeling, in others, it insensibly moulded popular feeling to suit its own requirements. He [Hall] accordingly avoided all controversy, preferring to rest quietly under imputations which he could not remove. In 1797, African Lodge assumed the prerogations of a Mother Lodge as "Kilwinning" did in Scotland; separating from the Mother Lodge, through force of circumstances, as did the "Royal York, of Friendship" at Berlin; and in imitation of the "Three Globes" at Berlin, and St. John's at Boston, raised itself to the dignity of a Grand Lodge. There are however, intimations that the original African Grand lodge was constituted by the concurrence of African Lodge, No. 459, Boston; African Lodge, No. 1 Philadelphia; and African (?) Lodge, No. 2, Rhode Island. The title *African* was a race, not an individual distinction, and its application was general and indiscriminate. When the necessity for the change became apparent, the general title *African* was dropped, and the Grand Lodge adopted the name of its eminent founder. It seems probable that this circumstance gave rise to the opinion of Mr. Moore and Mr. Gardner, that after the death of Prince Hall the Lodge became extinct. We have so far anticipated the progress of Masonry among black men, that we omitted to mention that African Lodge, after mature deliberations, petitioned the Grand Lodge of Massachusetts for the privilege of affiliation. The records do not show that any reply was elicited, and it is fair to presume that the petition found its way into the wastebasket. By making this proposal they raised nothing; yet it was a proposition which their opponents could not squarely reject without assuming all of the responsibility attending such an act.

The black Masons could not sacrifice an iota of their ancient and inherent privileges by uniting with another body of Masons; nor could they be outlawed by any power whatsoever for obeying what the common law had time after time pronounced to be just and lawful. While this measure was pending, the proposition for the abolition of slavery was before the people. American law from the highest tribunal in the Commonwealth struck off the shackles from the bondment; but Masonic equity, blind to the necessity of an amelioration, refused to entertain the petition of black Masons. The Massachusetts Grand Lodge did not choose to assume any such responsibility, and the matter was suffered to rest in abeyance.

From and after its independence, Prince Hall Grand Lodge continued to make progress, moving on "in the even tenor of her way," and it is a creditable fact, that the policy of this Grand Lodge has not been materially changed since the days of its founder. There has been no unusual display of zeal in organization of new Lodges, no effort to compete with, or outstrip daughter Grand Lodges; but with a fixed purpose to inculcate and perpetuate the genuine principles of the Order there has been a constant striving to penetrate into deeper truths, and to fully comprehend the aims and purposes of its teachings. There has been a steady intellectual growth, and as distinct connected historical information respecting the origin of Freemasonry among black men had not been brought to light, this Mother Lodge has accepted the task as her special mission. Besides the charters granted to four Lodges in Massachusetts, several were subsequently sent to Pennsylvania, and, in 1837, a memorable year in the history of black Freemasons, a Grand Lodge of black Masons was organized upon the three Lodge theory at Philadelphia.

The Grand Lodge of Pennsylvania was formed by the concurrence of three Lodges, and assumed the title of the "Hiram Grand Lodge of Pennsylvania." This became a healthy and vigorous organization, and many daughter Lodges were established in its own State, and in Ohio. Ten years subsequent, another Grand Lodge was formed in Pennsylvania under the title of the "First Independent African Grand Lodge of North America." Both of these, together with Prince Hall Grand Lodge, were represented in Boston in 1847, at the formation of the "National Grand Lodge," and the following year, 1848, the younger was merged into the older. From the "Hiram Grand Lodge," we trace the Grand Lodge of Ohio, herself the Mother Lodge of Missouri and Illinois, as we have elsewhere endeavored to show. A few months subsequent to the union of the two Pennsylvania Grand Lodges, the element which was before known as the "Hiram Grand Lodge," cancelled its assent to the union, withdrew from its obligation to the "Compact" and has since remained independent under the title of "The Grand Lodge of Pennsylvania." The other element maintained its organization, and has been regarded as the corner stone of the National Compact, furnishing during successive years its Grand Master and Grand Secretary.

It is claimed that the "missing records" have been recently recovered, which makes some important changes in the line of investigation we have pursued; that the first Independent African Grand Lodge, antedates the Hiram organization more than twenty years, and that this organization is even older than the Prince Hall Grand Lodge.
*(See our notice of Penn.*[10]*)*

The objections to black Masons were formerly based upon the word "freeborn." The position was considered impregnable, because the expression occurred in the English constitution. American Masons reasoned with Judge Taney that there are "slave races," that black men were by right as well as by law, slaves, and that they could never be participators in the institutions intended for the benefit and happiness of white men. This was the generally accepted sentiment of American Masons, and they knew no "higher law." In 1837, a Lodge in Canada submitted to the Grand Lodge of Scotland, its Mother Lodge, the important question, "whether emancipated slaves could share in the privileges of Freemasons." After mature deliberation, that Grand Lodge walked by Masonic Light to the sublime conclusion, *that the expression 'freeborn,' meant a person who was free at the time of his becoming a member of the Lodge, his own master, and sovereign disposer of his own title and actions.*

This interpretation was also affirmed by the Grand Orient of France and the Grand Lodge of England. This was emphatically a settlement of the whole question under dispute, viz: The fitness of the black man for the enjoyment of the privileges of Masonry. We cannot see that the issue is materially changed, because, forced to abandon one theory, our opponents embrace one equally absurd. Theories mislead, principles only are vital living realities. We have no hesitation then, in affirming as our settled conviction, that the issue of this question will be the partial or entire destruction of the doctrine of territorial jurisdiction. Each fact in the development of our history, has only helped us on to this conclusion. We walked by faith, timidly but hopefully, to the goal of recognition when the first clash of the revolution broke upon our astonished ears; now we walk to it by sight, boldly, and without fear of disappointment. We may be slow in reaching it. Great social proscriptions do not, ordinarily, either come or go in a day. And yet the perpetual changes which have been rung upon "freeborn, " irregularity and territorial jurisdiction are such as to inspire the disgust of all reflecting men. And the unwarrantable concealments and misrepresentations which have been made use of to preclude the truth, are of a nature to excite the condemnation of all honest men.

We now close our examination into the *origin, growth and progress of Freemasonry among black men.* We have brought it down to the first two black organizations, from which all others have a clear line of descent. We would gladly have traced more in detail, but we have exhausted the information at our command. We ask ourselves at this point whether, in these remarks, our case has been satisfactorily vindicated from the aspersions thrown upon it; and whether it has been shown to be worthy of the advocacy of our friends, and the consideration of our opponents. Every Mason is bound to answer these questions for himself, in accordance with the promptings of his conscience and understanding, and act by the dictates of his temperate judgment. Nothing can absolve him from this duty. It is not one to which he is constrained by all the obligations that connect the society together, and to discharge sincerely and conscientiously. No partial motive, no pride of opinion, no temporary feeling or prejudice will justify an improper judgment. Let him avoid an obstinate adherence to caste; and let him remember that Freemasonry cannot cling to the delusions of the past when religion, law, politics, and all human institutions are on the upward march.

Icarus, having to cross the sea by flight, was commanded by his father that he should neither fly too high nor too low, for his wings being joined with wax, if he should mount too high, it was to be feared the wax would melt by the heat of the sun, and if too low, lest misty vapors of the sea would make it less tenacious; but he, with youthful impulse, soared too high, fell down headlong and perished in the water. The application is easy and natural. Duty lies in a direct path between the extremes of injury and injustice. Let no impulse prompt American Masons to either of these; let them seek diligently the path of duty, there is the goal, there is safety.[11]

18. **What is today, the most pressing concern of Prince Hall Freemasonry?**

The issue of regularity! The standards of regularity accepted today would place all Masonic powers, other than the

Grand Lodge of England itself, outside of the pale of regularity. Most so-called mainstream Masonic historians who point an accusing finger at Prince Hall Freemasonry and call it irregular or clandestine, accept their Grand Lodges as being regular and refuse to use the same standards by which they judge Prince Hall Freemasonry. They simply turn a blind eye or overlook the truth.

The first black United States Senator Hiram Rhodes Revels, a Prince Hall Freemason, wrote in 1858 something that continues to have a lot of meaning even to this day:

*"We so far, with such historical data as we at present can reach, can see no essential difference between the course of our colored Lodges and the primary American Grand Lodges of our pale brethren. If, therefore, they cannot affiliate with us, we beg of them not hastily to condemn us. We feel that whilst they condemn us, they must condemn themselves, to a great degree."*[12]

It is sad, that there is a silent majority within mainstream American Freemasonry which allows a vocal minority to be their spokesman. Basically, most of those who make up that silent majority, are good and true men, who would be willing to reach an accord with Prince Hall Freemasonry and end the long night of madness that continues to separate our two Masonic powers.

Some in the leadership positions within the mainstream have approached the subject, but did not have the backbone to take the necessary steps to bring American Freemasonry out of its dark ages and into the light. Some have used all types of dodges, parries and side-steps to avoid the great issues facing American Freemasonry.

As an example, in answer to an open letter from members of his Grand Lodge, one Grand Master responded:

"I want now to speak to you about a matter which has concerned this Grand Lodge for many years. I have reference to our relationship to Negro Masonry. Our continuing committee of Past Grand Masters appointed to study Negro Masonry in the United States has the subject constantly in mind. I know that in some areas of our Grand Jurisdiction there exists an interest in our relationship with Negro Masonry, especially Prince Hall Masonry.

"I believe that the interest of our Lodges and of our members is increasing and I am not surprised that it does gain some impetus because of our increased awareness of the basic justice of civil rights.

"The problem, however, is not easily solved, nor easily defined. There are some who urge that we re-affirm our resolution of 1947. Some think that we should Masonically recognize Prince Hall Masonry into our Grand Lodge structure as a Provincial Grand Lodge, and there are those who argue for the *status quo* which permits a man, whatever his color, to make application for membership in Masonry and be accepted if found worthy.

"As with civil rights, our country is Masonically divided in its reactions to the recognition of Negro Masonry. We cannot view without dismay the prospect of Masonic disharmony in this country, whatever its cause. Relationships between Grand Jurisdictions are best developed and preserved at the level of the Grand lodge in each jurisdiction.

"Representatives of a number of Jurisdictions that share this Masonic problem have met on two occasions to exchange views and to consider possible actions and reactions. I have made every effort as your Grand Master to foster harmony between our Grand Lodge and all those which I have visited. My efforts have been to discover whether a united approach is possible to the common problem of the Grand Lodges in the states in which Negro Masonry exists, and to develop a tolerant attitude among the other Grand Lodges which will result in a Masonic understanding of any future action which our Grand Lodge might take.

"With Massachusetts our relationship with Prince Hall Masonry has been until recently at the Grand Lodge level. Our committee on Negro Masonry, consisting of our presiding and Past Grand Master, has held two fraternal and mutually helpful dinner meetings with the Prince Hall Grand Master and some of his Past Grand Masters and Officers. In the spring of this year, I invited M.W. Brother William E. Reed, Grand Master of Prince Hall Masonry in Massachusetts, to still another dinner under similar circumstances. It was decided to postpone it until fall and on September 4, I extended another invitation.

"I hope that this information will indicate to you the extent of my interest and concern, and that of all our Grand lodge officers, I ask for your indulgence in attempting to arrive at the solution which will be best for Massachusetts Masonry and for Masonry in the entire United States, and will be just and Masonically equitable to our Negro Brethren.

"This can best be done, and must be done, at the Grand Lodge level. If our constituent Lodges became involved or communicate with the Grand Lodges of other jurisdictions, whether recognized or not recognized, without a full knowldge of what has already been done, they are working at cross purposes to our Grand Lodge and may be performing a disservice to the other Grand Lodges. I call your attention to Section 703 of the Grand Constitution which reads as follows:

*Interjurisdictional correspondence shall in all cases be conducted through the office of the Grand Master except as he may otherwise order.*

"At this time I request, in the hope that it will not be necessary for me to enjoin, our constituent Lodges, their officers and members, to strictly observe the provisions of Section 703 and to refrain from communicating either officially or unofficially on Masonic matters with any unrecognized Grand Lodge, or with its subordinate Lodges, their officers or members. It is fundamental Masonic law of long standing that such communication be conducted by the respective Grand Lodges.

"I strongly urge our constituent Lodges to feel free to tell the Grand Master of their concern or hope for action on any matter at any time, but I must request that no

Lodge enter upon a program of circularizing other constitutent Lodges or urging concerted actions with such Lodges on the matter of Negro Masonry."[13]

Yet, there remains hope. In a recent unpublished paper by Christopher Haffner of Hong Kong, there seems to be one solution. He writes "We today continue to recognize and in the past have recognized as regular, many Grand Lodges that do not meet our present day standards. The only way that regularity of origin can be judged is by looking at the acceptable standards of the time. It seems to be a general rule that no Mason has ever been willing to admit 'I am irregular' but has been all too ready to accuse others. This has often resulted in reinforcement of those barriers which Masonry was constituted to overcome."

Bro. Haffner continues by suggesting some minor rephrasing of his Grand Lodge's *Basic Principles of Grand Lodge Recognition*, and instead of "...by a duly recognized Grand Lodge or by three or more regularly constituted Lodges" should be replaced by "... in such a manner as to maintain a historical descent from the originial Grand Lodges of the British Isles."

Another important principle is that, whilst regularity of origin may seriously affect recognition, it need not affect negotiations directed towards masonic unity. "...when one Grand Lodge has affected a presumed superiority, even if partly justified, union negotiations have broken down or the result has not been lasting. To force a brother to admit that he is less regular than another as the price of unity is a heavy toll to extract from anyone, when his motivation for negotiating is that he loves and practices the masonry into which he was himself initiated."

Bro. Haffner records seven categories as a suggested recognition of the reality that life, even Masonic Life, does not consist solely of right and wrong. He calls it "graded recognition."

1. *Clandestine* This means that the so-called Masonic body has no real relationship to freemasonry. Either it is so

called by broadest analogy, e.g., the "Chinese Freemasons" descended from triad societies, or it consists of bodies which do not possess the three degrees or, in particular, lack the Hiramic legend. Members of these organizations are to be treated as if they were not Masons, except that before initiation they must call off such an allegiance. No union as equal Grand Lodges is possible, and the only form of union would be for whole lodges to be initiated as a group by dispensation. Whilst this category is universally accepted as existing, I would suggest that use of the word "Clandestine" should be restricted to describe those who have no claim whatsoever to be called Freemasons.

2. *Unrecognized* Bodies in this category have the essential three degrees and Hiramic legend but have departed from the basic principles of the craft in a fundamental manner, such as by admitting atheists or women, permitting discussion of politics or religion in their lodges, etc.

Union is only possible with such bodies following a clear declaration that they will no longer depart form these principles, and that no atheists or women remain as members. Similarly, whole lodges and individual masons can be admitted into Grand Lodge and lodge membership respectively on so declaring, without being reinitiated. No recognition of the existence of such jurisdictions need be made in forming new lodges, etc. An example is the Grand Orient of France.

3. *Irregular* Bodies in the category are irregular in minor respects, e.g., they require belief in a Supreme Being but do not display the VSL, or they concurrently occupy the same territory as a "regular" Grand Lodge but have no treaty with it. These bodies can negotiate as equals in any Union negotiations. Inter-visitation is permitted when union negotiation and on other specific occasions by dispensation, e.g., for consecrations and installations. However, joining membership would require a call off from the irregular jurisdiction and a special declaration. The territory of such

a Grand Lodge is not open except in the case of coexistence with another Grand lodge regarded as regular. This category would seem to equate with the "Treaty of Intervisitation" concept of some of the Latin American Grand Lodges.

4. *Unrepresented*. This category can be characterized as a Grand Lodge which is regular in all but minor respects, or is fully regular but lacks support in some way, such as having predominatly non-national membership. The only difference between such a Grand Lodge and other represented Grand Lodges would lie in its right to exchange representatives and, as a consequence, the right to wear Grand Lodge regalia and be saluted in one another's meetings. Whilst this intermediate category is not practiced, the existence of Grand Lodges which do not exchange representatives make its extension into a category of less than full recognition possible.

5. *Represented*. A Grand Lodge recognized on a fully equal basis with representatives exchanged at Grand Lodge level. Examples abound, and this is the normal situation between regular, sovereign Grand Lodges.

6. *Concordant* Grand Lodges which are not only represented fully equal, but also by concordat have special agreements regarding the nature of Freemasonry, the extent of their jurisdictions, notification of expulsions, etc.

Examples are: the *Aims & Relationships* of the 1939; the Concordat of 1905 between the Grand Lodges of the British Isles; the conclusions reached by the Grand Masters Conference of North America; the *Concordat* between Massachusetts and Panama about lodges in the Canal Zone, etc.

7. *Unified*. This last category which I suggest is distinct from that of being united in one Grand Lodge, is the example set by Germany, whose United Grand Lodges elect a single Grand Master, etc., but retain much of the identity of the earlier separate Grand Lodges. This category is treated for all recognition purposes as if it were a single

Grand Lodge; it forms perhaps the greatest potential for union in Latin America.[14]

Bro. Haffner further explains "It seems to me there are a number of advantages to be gained from having a graded list such as this. Approval or disapproval of specific acts of other Grand Lodges can be reflected in such a way as to encourage greater conformity to stardards of regularity. Immediate recognition and encouragement of a new Grand Lodge is possible without the need to see how it works out. Negotiations can be carried out towards union and concordats without the negotiators feeling that they are restrained from visitation at the same time, so that the dignity and content of the other body's Masonic ceremonial can be examined at first hand. The list of advantages could be extended without difficulty."

"But the greatest advantage," continues Haffner, "of this concept might lie in its ability to partly overcome one problem of unity: that of the recognition of the new united Grand Lodge which has just resulted from two separate bodies. Clearly each is going to wish for those bodies which it previously recognized to continue to be recognized by the united body. This could well involve two separate Grand Lodges in some other territory which still do not recognize each other. If the union is to be conducted as between equals, neither can have precedence. A temporary downgrading of recognition from *represented* to *unrepresented* from both bodies might be a solution to such a problem."

Perhaps American Freemasonry can adopt procedures along Bro. Haffner's suggestions. For more than 200 years we have maintained the most segregated institution in America: racism and racial antagonism having sway, creating a situation that is intolerable, un-Masonic and un-American. A solution must be found. Perhaps Bro. Haffner's guidelines may hold the key.

Perhaps.

# Notes For Part Five

1. Harold V.B. Voorhis: *Negro Masonry in the United States* and Harry A. Williamson: *Prince Hall Masonry in New York State.*

2. Harry A. Williamson: *A Brief History of Negro Masonry;* Commemoration of the 125th Anniversary of the Lodge of St. Andrew, November 30, 1881, pages 59/61; and *Proceedings* of Grand Lodge of Massachusetts (white), 1871, page 252.

3. *Proceedings* from the Grand Lodge of Illinois (white) 1889, Appendix Part I, page 158 and pages 162/162; Harold V. B. Voorhis: *Negro Masonry in the United States,* page 43; *Proceedings* of the Grand Lodge of Massachusetts (white) 1889, Appendix VI, pages 454/463; and *Proceedings* of the Grand Lodge of Washington (white), 1899, Vol. XIII, Part I, Appendix, page 99.

4. Harry A. Williamson: *A Brief History of Negro Masonry,* and *Proceedings* of the Grand Lodge of Michigan (white), 1874, page 56 and page 87.

5. *The New England Craftsman,* Boston, Mass., August 1912, page 36.

6. *Proceedings* of the Grand Lodge of Illinois (white) 1899, Appendix, Part I, page 138 and pages 161/162.

7. *Proceedings* of the Grand Lodge of Ohio (white) 1870, page 24 and pages 41/42.

8. *Proceedings* of the Grand Lodge of New York (white) 1791/1852.

9. *Proceedings* of the Grand Lodge of Ohio (white) 1876.

10. From the proceedings of the Semi-Annual Communciation of June 24th, 1874,...this interesting extract:

> *"The Committee to search for Missing Records reported having found the following books and documents, all of which they take great pleasure in handing over to the Grand Lodge:*
>
> *1. Minute book of the organization of the First Independent African Grand Lodge, from the 28th of December, 1815, to December 9th, 1817.*
>
> *2. A minute book from September 19th, 1845, to January 17th, 1848.*
>
> *3. Cash book of the Grand Lodge form 1850 to 1859.*
>
> *4. A warrant of the organization of the First Independent African Grand Lodge, bearing date December 28th, 1815.*

5. *Minute book from March 6th, 1848, to December 5th, 1860. Report on Foreign Correspondence, Grand Lodge of Missouri 1876, page 83.*

11. Willis N. Brent: *Ibid*

12. Joseph A. Walkes, Jr.: *Black Square & Compass: 200 Years of Prince Hall Freemasonry*, (Virginia, Macoy, 1981) page 94.

13. *Quarterly Communication of the M.W. Grand Lodge (white) of Massachusetts*, September 10, 1969, page 261.

14. Christopher Haffner, *Regularity of Origin*, unpublished.

# Addendum
## The Phylaxis Society
### A Look at the Organization and its Relationship with Regular Freemasonry

Within the 250,000 member Prince Hall Masonic fraternity, that sustains Masonic lodges in the United States, Canada, South America, Liberia (West Africa), the Republic of Panama, and the Bahamas, along with a large number of military lodges wherever there is an American military presence, has grown an interesting and noteworthy Masonic research organization.

Its membership application reads in part that it is "an international organization of Prince Hall Freemasons who seek light and who have light to impart." It further explains "the Society provides a universal center and bond of union for Prince Hall Freemasons everywhere who desire to pursue the study of Masonry, receive light and disperse light," while emphasizing "it will in no way interfere with the legislative and ritualistic affairs of any Masonic body." With that statement of purpose, the applicant who submits his request for membership in the Phylaxis Society (pronounced Fi Lak Sis) will enter into the stimulating and challenging adventure of Masonic education.

While membership is limited to Prince Hall Freemasons, "regular" Freemasons find that they are welcomed as subscribers and, as this article will show, play a most interesting role.

To better understand its concept, one must have some understanding of its name, and the importance its Organization attaches to it.

The Society adopted as its name a suitable, but loosely defined Greek term having a dual meaning—"to preserve and safeguard." A description the group takes seriously and around which the Organization has been structured.

In the beginning it emulated to some degree the fifty year old successful Philalethes Society using it as its role model. The new Society adopted the basic organization structure of that group. For instance, like its older counterpart, the officers are widely scattered about the country. At present the President (and founder) resides in Leavenworth, Kansas; the 1st Vice President, in Tacoma, Washington; the 2nd Vice President, in Brooklyn, New York; the Treasurer, in Tacoma, Washington; the Editor of its *Phylaxis Magazine* in Boston (Roxbury), Massachusetts; a *Phylaxis Newsletter* Editor in Detroit, Michigan; and a European Representative in Frankfurt, Germany.

Between the two groups, the *Philalethes* and the *Phylaxis*, the similarity is often striking, such as the initials carried behind the members' names, but there the similarity ends. For instance, the *Phylaxis* Society adopted as its symbol, the square and compass resting on an open book, over the lamp of knowledge, which was similar in some respect to an older design used by the *Philalethes*. However, the *Phylaxis* society inserted the number "15," as a measure of its dedication to its Fraternity.

A matter of much speculation within Masonic circles, the number "15," is a representation of the very nature of the Society and its various programs, though like the Organization's name, having a dual significance. On the one hand it serves as a reminder of "Prince Hall," the founder of the Order, and the fourteen Blacks who became the first of their race to be initiated into Freemasonry; while on the other hand, it also represents the number of "actual" Fellows, authorized by society.

Fellows earn this title by writing a thesis dubbed "Masterpiece" on some aspect of Prince Hall Freemasonry, publishing it in the Society's magazine and hence receiving a "Certificate of Fellow" with the additional possibility of being nominated for the highly coveted "Certificate of Literature." Within the eight years of its existence, this literature certificate has only been awarded five times; four of the members having published a book on Prince Hall Freemasonry, such as the well-known historian Dr. Charles H. Wesley, whose work *Prince Hall: Life and Legacy* was published in 1977, and Joseph A.

Walkes, Jr., whose book *Black Square & Compass: 200 Years of Prince Hall Freemasonry* was first released in 1979, and reprinted by Macoy in 1981.

While the "Actual" Fellows are limited to fifteen in number, the Society awards "Honorary" Fellow status to those who have made outstanding contributions to Prince Hall Freemasonry and the Society. This program is also unique because it is awarded to Prince Hall and "regular" Freemasons as well. It is probably one of the few occasions in American Freemasonry that members of both fraternities come together in a common but non-official endeavor. "Regular" Freemasons who are "Honorary" Fellows of the *Phylaxis* Society are:

Keith Arrington, retired Assistant Librarian of the Iowa Masonic Library.

Jerry Marsengill, Editor, *The Philalethes* and the *Royal Arch Mason*.

L. Sherman Brooks, Masonic calligrapher from New York who has done a number of covers for the *Phylaxis Magazine*.

Allen E. Roberts, Editor, *The Altar Light*, author, film producer and Masonic educator.

George Draffen of Newington, Grand Lodge of Scotland.

While this program marks a unique approach within American Freemasonry, it is just one of the many singular features of the Organization. The Society goes one step further by awarding a special "Certificate of Literature" named after one of its mentors, Ira S. Holder, Sr., an elderly Prince Hall Masonic historian from New York. This certificate is awarded to those outside of the Prince Hall Masonic organization.

"Regular" Freemasons having received this honor have been George Draffen of Newington for his paper, "Prince Hall Freemasonry" which appeared in *Ars Quatuor Coronatorum, Transactions of Quatuor Coronati Lodge No. 2076* (Vol. 89, 1977) and Raymond H. Draget of Connecticut, for his paper "Prince Hall Freemasonry in the United States of America," published by Philosophic Lodge of Research A.F.& A.M.

Two women writers, neither connected to any of the American adoptive rites such as the Eastern Star, were also honored for works on the Prince Hall Fraternity: Mrs. Alfredteen Harrison, author of "A History of the Most Worshipful Stringer Grand Lodge: Our History is our Challenge," and Dr. Loretta J. Williams, author of "Black Freemasons and Middle-class Realities." Ms. Harrison is a Professor of History and Dr. Williams a Professor of Sociology.

The Society publishes a number of items. Its hallmark being the *Phylaxis Magazine*, published every three months and received by members and subscribers around the world. Like the Society itself, it is considered to be the most unique publication within Prince Hall Freemasonry. Like similar publications dedicated to Masonic research, history and education, the magazine carries articles on all aspects of Freemasonry in general and Prince Hall Freemasonry in particular. A number of "regular" Freemasons have had articles published in the *Phylaxis:* Keith Arrington, Harvey Newton Brown, Alphonse Cerza, George Draffen, the late Conrad Hahn, Jerry Marsengill, Allen E. Roberts, Harold V.B. Voorhis, to name but a few.

Some articles appearing within its pages have sparked numerous debates. For instance, during the Bi-Centennial fever that held sway throughout the country in 1976, was carried an opposing discussion: "Should Prince Hall Masons celebrate the Bi-Centennial?" "A resounding yes!" by Jerry Marsengill of the *Philalethes* Society and "An Adamant No!" by Joseph A. Walkes, Jr. the President of the *Phylaxis* Society.

Some time later the magazine carried "The Power and the Glory: An in depth look at Prince Hall Masonry," an introduction to a larger on-going research project. The article a "Masterpiece" submitted by the Society's Executive Secretary became an overnight subject of discussion within Prince Hall Masonry, firing up heated debates, applauded by some, condemned by others. The article was so contested by one member, a Grand Master, that he refused to renew his membership in protest. However, at the time of this writing, several years after the publication, he has rejoined the ranks of active membership within the Society. Lately, a series of articles has also drawn considerable interest in the Masonic world of Philately, and has been responsible for a large influx of letters to the Society. The article, "Prince Hall Freemasonry and Postage Stamps," written by the President of the Society has been very well received and in some respects, opening new grounds for those who collect stamps related to Masonry.

Each March is published a special issue of the magazine in commemoration of the initiation of Prince Hall: March 6th, 1775, with the issue geared to one particular subject. In 1979 it was "The literature of Prince Hall Freemasonry," in 1980: "The Order of the Eastern Star." It is with this issue the Society publishes the "Prince Hall Credo" and its annual statement concerning its approach to recognition.

While the main thrust of the Society is the printing and distribution of its magazine, it also publishes a supplement, *The Phylaxis Newsletter* which is printed twice a year. The newsletter carries news of the membership, the activities of the various Chapters and reports of the Society's annual Executive Session. Both of these publications are distinct from each other and carry two different editors.

The Society also publishes its Transactions called *"Lux e Tenebris"* (Light Out of Darkness), when authorized by the Executive Committee. It not only carries the minutes of the Society's annual meeting and the papers read before it, but also contains out-of-print works as well. The latest Transactions carries the full text of the classic *Negro Mason in Equity* by Samuel W. Clark originally appearing in 1886.

While the various activities already listed are numerous, there remain other areas in which the Society is involved. After the death of the Sovereign Grand Commander of the United Supreme Council, A.A.S.R., Southern Jurisdiction (PHA), who was also an Honorary Fellow, the Society minted a medal in his likeness, and annually presents "The John G. Lewis, Jr., Medal of Excellence," to those who meet the high standards set by the Society. The medals are donated by Grand Lodges, lodges and interested individuals in support of the program.

The Society continues its commemoration of Prince Hall by meeting as close to March the 6th as possible, usually the entire first week of the month. Unlike the *Philalethes* Society which usually meets in Washington D.C., each year the *Phylaxis* Society meets in its annual "Executive Session" at different locations across the country.

The requirements as set forth by the Society are that they must receive an invitation from a Grand Lodge and be hosted by a Chapter of the Society. The Chapter takes on the responsiblity for making all of the necessary arrangements for the annual session. At present the Society has fifteen Chapters, two being "special," one composed of editors and the other of historians.

At these annual sessions all is not just geared to receiving reports, as considerable effort is stressed on taking tours of the various Masonic institutions, both Prince Hall and "regular," in the area. Over the years the Society has visited a number of institutions maintained by "regular" Freemasonry such as the Masonic Temple of the Grand Lodge of Massachusetts A.F. & A.M.; The Iowa Masonic Library, Museum and Administration Building of the Grand Lodge of Iowa A.F. & A.M.; The Masonic Temple in Tacoma; the Grand Lodge of Washington F. & A.M. in Seattle; and the magnificent Masonic Temple of the Grand Lodge of Michigan F.& A.M. in Detroit, as well as a number of Scottish Rite temples of the Mother Supreme Council of the World. Many of the tours taken by the Society are of major historical importance, bringing the Prince Hall Masons to their roots. For instance, in 1976 they were able to view Charter 459 of African Lodge granted by the Grand Lodge of England and maintained in a bank vault in Boston by the Prince Hall Grand Lodge of Massachusetts, as well as visit the grave site and monument to Prince Hall at the famous Copps Hill Burial ground.

During the 1981 session, the members crossed into Canada: to Dresden, Ontario to visit the grave site of Bro. Josiah Henson whose early life in slavery provided much of the material for Harriet Beecher Stowe's novel Uncle Toms Cabin. Henson, who became a Prince Hall Freemason, had escaped from slavery in 1830 in Upper Canada and, in 1841, he and a group of abolitionist purchased 200 acres in the vicinity of his grave site.

An article, "Rev. Josiah Henson, Uncle Tom and Prince Hall Freemasonry" had been published in the *Phylaxis* Magazine.

Upon paying their respects to Bro. Henson, the members proceeded to North Buston, Ontario, to the Raleigh Township where is located the Centennial Museum and memorial to the Elgin Settlement, a haven for slaves in the pre-Civil War years. There the members were able to see numerous artifacts of slavery as well as a rich collection of the Prince Hall Masonic experience in the area. Tours such as these are stressed by the Society for their Masonic educational value.

Not content with tours, the Society makes it a point to schedule a visit to a Prince Hall Lodge in session. In some instances lodges are granted dispensations by their Grand Lodges to hold special meetings so the visiting members of the Society can view their work. This has had its lighter moments. Once, a very nervous newly elected Worshipful Master received the Grand Masters, the Sovereign Grand Commander of the Southern Jurisdiction and various other Grand Lodge officers who were attending the society's meeting.

While the tours are pleasant educational experiences, the highlight of the annual meeting is the workshop/seminar hosted by the *Phylaxis* Society. The various workshops usually run eight hours and cover a multitude of Masonic subjects. However, several are on-going and permanent and presented each year. Masonic History, The Masonic Magazine; Its Role in the Educational Process, Non-Prince Hall Masonry in the Phylaxis Society are standard workshops assigned to the Executive Staff. The Society plans to begin an eight hour Masonic leadership course based on Allen E. Roberts' book *Key to Freemasonry's Growth* and the "More Light in Masonry" series. This course of instruction is complete with films, work books, and certificate of training at the end of the course.

It was briefly mentioned at the start of this article that one interpretation of "Phylaxis" was to preserve. Nowhere is this better exemplified than in the Masonic Hall of Fame maintained by the Society. This "vehicle" is used to pay homage to those Freemasons of the past who made worthwhile contributions, usually in the field of literature, but not restricted to that singular expression, to Prince Hall Freemasonry. Each year three names are chosen, two Prince Hall and one "regular" Freemason, to be "enshrined" by the Society.

In honor of those named to the Phylaxis Hall of Fame, a certificate and plaque is presented to the selectees' Grand Lodges. "Regular" Freemasons so honored have been P.G.M. William H. Upton of the Grand Lodge of the State of Washington, author of *Negro Masonic Being a Critical Examination* (1902) as well as other works on Prince Hall Freemasonry; and Josef G. Findel, the German Masonic historian who carried the title of Honorary Past Grand Master of the Prince Hal Grand Lodge of Massachusetts and European Representative of Prince Hall Freemasonry. It is expected that over the years some 25 "regular" Freemasons' names will be engraved alongside of their Prince Hall Masonic brethren onto the rolls of the Masonic Hall of Fame.

As the two thousand member Society closes in on its first decade, like any new organization, it has had its growing pains, made its share of mistakes, but happy in the knowledge that they were from the heart rather than from the head. The Society looks ahead to the future and years of service not only to the Prince Hall Fraternity but to all Freemasonry.

The *Phylaxis* Society and Prince Hall Freemasonry recognize themselves as being a branch of "regular" Freemasonry, and the the term "Regular' as used in this article, is used only to designate that branch which is not of the Prince Hall designation.

JOSEPH A. WALKES, JR.

1981